A JOHN CATT PUBLICATION

THE THINKING SCHOOL

Developing a dynamic
learning community

Dr Kulvarn Atwal

First published 2019

by John Catt Educational Ltd,
15 Riduna Park, Station Road,
Melton, Woodbridge IP12 1QT

Tel: +44 (0) 1394 389850 Fax: +44 (0) 1394 386893
Email: enquiries@johncatt.com
Website: www.johncatt.com

ISBN: 978 1 912 906 02 4

Set and designed by John Catt Educational Limited

Acknowledgements

I would like to take the opportunity to thank my inspirational wife and children for all their support and encouragement.

Big thanks to Sandeep and Rachel for taking the time to read my near-final drafts. Thanks to Jean and Gerry for enabling me to complete my research.

I would like to thank every amazing professional and child that I have ever worked with for inspiring me to write this book.

Contents

Chapter 1

Why we need
a thinking school

I am certain that teachers enter the profession because they want to make a positive difference to children's lives. My experience as an educator has taught me that the primary job for leaders in schools is to enable teachers to succeed in this aim. This book is based on the simple premise that the greatest influence on the quality of children's learning experiences in schools is the quality of teaching, and I doubt that anyone would disagree with that. However, I also think that the greatest influence on the quality of teaching is the quality of teacher learning experiences. This is where there is considerable room for improvement in our schools.

This book presents a model for improving the quality of teacher learning experiences in schools, and consequently improving children's learning and progress. Ironically, in the institutions where the core business is learning, the quality of teacher learning experiences is poor. This anomaly has inspired my work. We need a thinking school because we need to reconceptualise the role of teachers in schools and our expectations for their workplace learning.

Imagine the best teacher you have ever seen or worked with. What makes them so great? So special? Equally, imagine the best school leader you have ever seen or worked with. What makes them so effective? What would your school be like if every teacher and every leader was as good as those you are imagining? What would the children's experiences be like in that school? Would every child, regardless of their background and learning needs, be flourishing academically, socially and emotionally? The thinking school is a learning organisation where all members of staff see themselves as both learners and leaders. They are all reflective, creative decision makers who understand that they are constantly developing and learning. Throughout the book, I will discuss the value of learning-focused leaders who are able to model teacher learning behaviours and mentor and coach colleagues.

In the thinking school, everyone is responsible for learning and teaching, and children's learning outcomes are central to every conversation. I have deliberately used the term 'thinking' because I want to capture the self-reflection and criticality the word implies. When I walk into a classroom, I look to evaluate the quality of children's thinking and engagement, as well as what may be produced on paper. I will also seek to evaluate the quality of teachers' engagement, thinking and self-reflection. Teachers make thousands of decisions every day. I am interested in the quality of self-reflection and evidence-based thinking that directly informs their decision-making. I want to enable teachers to have opportunities to develop an explicit understanding of the tacit knowledge that informs their decision-making.

I have been a headteacher for six years (in my schools, my title is Head Learning Leader). I am aware that it is an extremely challenging role. I expect those challenges to increase in the next few years, with raised expectations for children's outcomes, recruitment difficulties and budget cuts on the horizon. My motivation for writing this book is to enable school leaders to meet these significant challenges in a way that is both cost effective to schools and empowering to all members of staff. Every member of staff within a school should be empowered to see themselves as a leader. This book is written for all teachers and educators as a model for schools to maximise the learning for every teacher and child. It is based on my personal experiences as a teacher and leader, and on the findings from my own research. I believe that the school in which I am privileged to work at present is a thinking school, and that every school can be one.

Teacher learning is important to me because I believe that we need innovative reflective teachers if we are to provide the best possible learning experiences for our children. This is of particular significance to our most vulnerable and disadvantaged children. Strong and confident teachers and leaders will be able to handle the challenges that schools continue to face to meet the individual learning needs of children and teachers. Headteachers have considerable responsibility in determining the learning and emotional climate at their schools. We need to be values-led and our leadership should be judged on our children's learning outcomes. The headteacher is the most important person at the school in living out and modelling its values, and these values need to include responsibility for teacher learning.

This book has grown out of a number of concerns and objectives:

- Ensuring that our teachers engage in quality learning experiences in their schools
- Supporting teachers in ongoing critical engagement in research
- Promoting teachers' wellbeing in schools and retaining teachers in the profession
- Promoting learning-focused leadership that ensures that leaders are judged by the quality of children's learning experiences
- The need for distributed leadership models in our schools and collaborative learning opportunities for all staff
- The need for creative, innovative risk-takers in our schools
- The urgent need to recruit and retain great teachers

Background to the study

I began my career as a primary school teacher in East London in 1999. Against the advice of senior colleagues, I began my Master's in Education (MA) in my first term as a newly qualified teacher (NQT). I did so primarily because I believed that I needed to continue to learn and engage in practical research if I was to develop as a teacher. I was actively discouraged by colleagues and the impression I was given at the time was that an MA was appropriate for a more senior or experienced teacher than an NQT. I ignored their advice and by the end of my third year, and having completed my MA, I was made responsible for the professional learning of all the teachers at the school. By this stage, I was convinced that teacher engagement in research was a model for their professional learning. Taking my own experiences in teaching as a starting point, I believed that our most effective teachers were those teachers who engaged in professional dialogue and reflection upon their practice, whether informally or formally, and who were prepared to implement change in their classroom as a result. I am talking about practitioners who take an active interest in educational issues and all the factors that potentially influence children's learning.

When I began my doctoral thesis in 2008, I was deputy headteacher and leader of all staff learning within the school in which I worked, one of the ten largest primary schools in England. My role required me to consider what strategies would have the greatest impact on an individual teacher's professional learning and their effectiveness within their role. I took this aspect of my job extremely seriously. Through undertaking a professional doctorate on teacher learning, I intended to reflect on the findings of my thesis to inform practice in both the schools I lead and beyond.

The purpose of my doctoral thesis was to explore the professional learning experiences of teachers in primary schools. I wanted to better understand the complex factors that influence the perceived quality of teacher learning in primary schools, and to arrive at a conceptualisation of what school leaders need to take into consideration when planning for teacher learning. I evaluated teachers' perceptions of these factors and drew on them to build a model to maximise teacher learning experiences. The findings in this book are therefore both evidence based and reflective of my own practical experience. I have taken into account the views of teachers as well as my own experience to develop the model for the thinking school, including specific strategies that can be implemented in schools to provide an expansive learning environment for all staff. This book is particularly timely because of the national context of challenges facing schools and school leaders. I am currently executive headteacher of two large primary schools in London. I believe that a headteacher should be seen as the lead learner at the school and

I have continued to explore all the formal and informal opportunities made available in the workplace to support learning.

The last decade has seen increasing recognition in schools and other organisations that attention needs to be given to staff professional development and growth (UCET, 2011; Cordingley et al., 2015). The findings in this book are therefore especially important because recent research evidence on teacher professional development (Eurydice, 2015) suggests that formal and traditional forms of in-service training, such as external courses and conferences, still prevail in almost all education systems. A central thread in my work is the value of examining current research from workplace learning and teacher learning literature in order to identify concrete ways to improve teacher learning experiences in schools.

In this book, I don't use the familiar initialism associated with teacher learning: CPD. Instead of Continuing Professional Development, I prefer to use professional learning or CPL. I believe it's worth emphasising the word 'learning' rather than 'development' to indicate that in the thinking school, teacher learning is as important and as valued as children's learning. I use CPL as an overarching term for all the activities teachers might be engaged in – formally or informally – that promote their learning. You will find examples including: teacher observation and modelling; team-teaching; external courses; professional learning meetings after school; coaching and mentoring; shadowing; networks within and across schools; collaborative learning; peer learning and lesson studies; professional reflection and engagement in teacher research.

Traditional experiences for teacher learning

My personal experiences of teacher professional learning over the last 18 years have been dominated by the need to *train* teachers to be able to implement government initiatives, instead of individualised professional *learning* opportunities. Another central thread through this book is the view that more learning is potentially undertaken informally by teachers in schools than through the formal opportunities designed for teacher learning. For example, there is greater potential to learn from colleagues in your year group team over the course of a week than from the one-hour professional learning meeting after school. Therefore we need to consider the learning environments in schools and evaluate the extent to which they maximise both formal and informal learning opportunities for teachers. An introduction to workplace learning theories, which I explore in detail later, elevated my thinking about teacher learning and opened my eyes to the possibility of creating a far more dynamic learning environment for all teachers within a school. This is central in the thinking school, and fundamental to improving children's learning experiences.

In contrast to the concepts of informal learning, my personal observations of teacher engagement in CPL seemed neither to deepen learning over time nor to promote collaborative learning amongst staff. Too much CPL is short term and not contextualised in practice. I am talking about courses or conferences off-site, usually organised by the local authority. Teachers perhaps valued the opportunity to have a day out of school but the impact back at school was slight, particularly in terms of wider teacher learning or children's learning outcomes. While I was working at a school in 2008 that was deemed to be struggling, representatives of the local authority were particularly dismissive of our intentions to promote teacher learning through action research. This demonstrated to me that there was a lack of wider awareness of the factors that actually influence teacher learning and development.

The situation was the same when I joined my current school as headteacher a few weeks after it had been categorised by Ofsted as 'requiring improvement'. I explained my determination and intention that all teachers would develop their understanding of the craft of learning and teaching and that we would do this through engagement in year group collaborative action research projects with learning-focused lesson observations. I was immediately informed that the teachers were not ready for this and that I needed to observe each teacher and give them a judgement of their teaching (a choice of 'unsatisfactory', 'requiring improvement', 'good' or 'outstanding') and targets for improvement. I refused and stuck with my original plan, even though I was told that Ofsted would return within 18 months and it was my job that was on the line. In leadership, you absolutely have to do what you believe is right.

I felt that these attitudes to school improvement were a reflection of the impact of government policy on promoting teacher learning through short-term externally developed courses. The notion presented by local authority advisors and external consultants was that action research would be 'more appropriate' for a school that was in a stronger position and more successful. I was told that it would be better to send teachers on one-day courses entitled 'From Good to Outstanding'. I am not discounting the fact that teachers can pick up worthwhile strategies from attending a generic course such as this. However, my own experiences suggest that teacher learning activities such as these seldom allow sufficient time for teachers to reflect on how any changes introduced impact on children's learning. Teachers also need to have the tools and the time to develop the skills to undertake this type of reflection effectively. Too many schools and teachers remain dependent on outside intervention to support their professional learning instead of exploiting the informal and formal learning opportunities available in every school. Many leaders in schools do not have the skills to develop the structures and cultures in schools to promote an expansive learning environment or to develop teachers' professional learning skills, including reflection upon practice. However, I do think all schools are capable of developing into thinking schools.

If, as I advocate in this book, we move towards professional learning communities within and across schools, we need to reconceptualise our views on what constitutes effective teacher professional learning. A recent study of international reviews of effective teacher professional learning (Cordingley et al., 2015) has highlighted the significance of sustained learning activities over time that additionally facilitate experimentation in the classroom. This requires us to change our understanding of the role of the teacher. I envisage each teacher in the thinking school to be a potential Master of Education who is actively engaging in research, continually experimenting to improve their craft year on year. If this is taking place within a wider environment of a professional learning community, the impact will be very powerful.

Situated approaches to learning

My work has been heavily influenced by workplace learning theories and it is useful to give you a background understanding of situated approaches to learning and communities of practice. I feel the education community has much to learn from this field of research about how to develop learning environments in schools that maximise formal and informal learning opportunities. The work of Lave and Wenger (1991) has been particularly significant in contributing to the development of theories of workplace learning as a social activity or situated theory of learning. Situated learning is about all the workplace learning that can take place informally in schools, and how we can purposefully create an environment which encourages staff to engage in informal learning. Think of formal learning as the one-hour-a-week staff meeting after school – we call them professional learning meetings (PLMs). Compare these to the various other opportunities during a working week that teachers may be learning informally, for example:

- Conversing with year group colleagues in partner classrooms about specific teaching strategies or individual children
- Conversing with colleagues across the school during the day or over lunch
- Reading magazine articles about education
- Reading websites/blogs about education
- Seeking out advice from colleagues with specialisms
- Marking books or assessments with colleagues
- Informal observations of teaching activities by colleagues, e.g. assemblies
- Team planning meetings
- Team-teaching
- Pupil progress meetings

In the foreword to Lave and Wenger's first text (1991), William Hanks discussed the innovative nature of their work, particularly the extent to which learning was located in the process of co-participation, and focused on the relationship between learning and the social situation in which it occurs. Learning through social activity has been featured in the literature on workplace learning more than it has been in the literature on teacher learning. There is significant additional potential for teachers to interact and learn socially in schools, and we can create an environment that encourages it. A recent example will demonstrate the potential for learning that can take place socially.

A newly qualified teacher (NQT) had a meeting with a parent which she had found difficult to manage, and came to see me informally during a break to discuss her concerns. Within a few moments, we happened to be joined by my deputy, the team leader for the year group, and the child's previous teacher. We decided to find time during our lunch break to support the NQT in co-constructing a written response, and an email was sent later that evening to the parent. It's a simple example, but it demonstrates how we have to create a culture in a school to enable this informal learning to thrive. All of us will have learned from this particular situation, but especially the NQT. She learned how to communicate effectively with parents. She also learned about the value of collaborative informal learning. Her response was to send an email to us that evening, outlining how great she felt to be 'part of such a strong support system'.

It is a useful exercise for educators in schools to think about pedagogy and how they believe children learn best. The next step is to consider the difference, if any, between the ways in which children learn best and how adults learn best. As a Head Learning Leader, I view the teachers' learning in the same way as I expect them to view their students' learning. In the same way that children's learning does not stop with the bell at the end of the school day, teachers' learning does not stop at the end of a training day or PLM. Learning should be a social experience for children and adults alike.

The findings presented in this book will demonstrate that the transferral of workplace learning literature supports school leaders in planning for teacher learning. Situated learning is widely accepted as a key component of professional education and practice in health and social care, so why not schools? It is particularly significant in signalling a move away from the views of traditional learning theorists who had conceptualised the learner as a receptacle of (taught) knowledge. I do acknowledge that 'direct instruction' is a legitimate form of teaching and learning, but I don't like to see learning in a classroom directed in such a finite way that children are regarded as empty vessels waiting to be filled with knowledge. I believe that children's talk is central to learning and that learning should be seen as social interaction within the classroom. Dialogue is at the centre of learning for children and adults alike, stimulating and extending thinking, engagement, learning and understanding, empowering all to be lifelong learners.

I would define situated learning not as training in the workplace but as learning in it. Whereas training describes the formal learning opportunities employers afford employees to learn new skills, situated learning encompasses a diverse range of learning which may or may not be formally structured. The traditional model of training is reflected in the apprenticeship model in industry and the experience of teachers going off-site to attend courses. Hodkinson and Hodkinson (2005) have discussed how Fordist forms of work organisation aimed to develop their workers to master specialised skills to complete specific tasks. The social aspects of collaborative learning or the personal growth of the learner were wholly irrelevant – this relates to the teacher who is sent out on a training course to develop a specific aspect of their practice without a thought for the social environment and context within which they work and learn.

I believe that the learning undertaken by teachers during these individual days out of school is easily forgotten on their return, and makes little impact on their practice. Situated learning is more encompassing, as it locates learning in social contexts at work. It recognises the importance of work experience and practical action in promoting learning. Lave and Wenger (1991) explain:

> 'In our view, learning is not merely situated in practice – as if it were some independently reifiable process that just happened to be located somewhere, learning is an integral part of generative social practice in the lived-in world'

This definition highlights the significance of workplace learning activities while engaged in social practice. It is this which directly facilitates professional learning opportunities. The significance of teachers' individual dispositions to learning is discussed in chapter 3. If teachers are to learn as an integral part of their practical experience in schools, they need to maintain a learning mentality. Do the teachers and leaders in your schools see themselves as lifelong learners, continually striving to develop their own and others' practice? The thinking school promotes an expansive learning environment that develops teachers' attitudes to learning – attitudes that in turn have a transformative effect, continually developing the learning environment. The reciprocal effect results in positive outcomes for children's learning. It sounds simple and it can be. I know that schools differ greatly in terms of the learning environments they provide and their propensity to afford quality learning opportunities for teachers, and also in terms of teacher and leader attitudes to learning.

Communities of practice

Lave and Wenger (1991) introduced the term 'communities of practice' to describe the learning that takes place as an integral dimension of social practice. Their original work on communities of practice through situated learning proposed the significance of active social participation as central to the learning process, and challenged the notion of formal education as represented by the traditional model of teacher-learner. If we transfer this to schools, we can reconceptualise our notion of how teachers learn at school and look beyond the formal contexts we provide and consider how we can create an environment that supports situated learning.

Taking this notion of communities of practice further, we can identify ways in which the learning community can reproduce itself. Working and belonging within this community contributes to the sense of identity of the workers and they consequently engage in learning within the social practices of the workplace and contribute to the learning of others. What this means in the thinking school is that each teacher's learning and growth is equally important to every teacher in the community, that teachers are learning and growing together, and that the community develops practice collaboratively. Returning to the earlier example of the NQT, she will have experienced the value of informal collaborative learning with colleagues. As she grows and develops, she will also provide informal support for others. The culture for informal learning will continue to grow. In schools, there is considerable scope for teachers to engage in social learning with colleagues. However, I have visited schools where this is clearly not the case, and there is a lack of a collaborative learning culture.

I noted early on in my research that the rich learning that therefore occurs within the normal social practices of the workplace contrasts greatly with the emphasis in schools for teachers to learn off-site or during the five in-service training (INSET) days designed specifically to support teacher learning. I noticed that it was the teachers that I considered to be the most effective who would often be seen engaged in informal professional dialogue with colleagues, discussing the needs of their students and aspects of learning and teaching. I became curious about how I could develop an environment in which professional dialogue was promoted and where all teachers had further opportunities to explore and discuss their practice. Part of my research then focused specifically on how a school could promote opportunities for this type of informal learning. I wanted to work in a school in which every teacher was like the most effective teacher that I had seen, with a passion and curiosity to continually improve, and focused entirely on children's learning outcomes.

Wenger (2008) has since discussed the value to schools of applying the concept of communities of practice, in terms of both teacher learning and pupil learning, and has cited the value of peer-to-peer professional learning activities. He argues that change will take longer in schools, as opposed to businesses, because a deeper transformation of conceptions of learning will have to take place. My own experiences in schools would indicate that a teacher could learn both through social participation in informal learning and through the formal teacher learning activities described. However, it is the quality of these formal professional learning opportunities, and the extent to which they are intellectually challenging and provide opportunities for reflection and learning over time, that is up for debate. I believe that formal activities (such as PLMs and INSET days) should provide as collaborative a learning experience as possible.

Opportunities for collaborative learning are essential. Leaders within schools make decisions that create or remove barriers to formal and informal learning activities and therefore influence the expansiveness of the learning environment. (For the purpose of this book, I use the term 'expansive' to indicate the extent to which the learning environment provides a wide range of quality learning opportunities for teachers.) A school can be described as a community of learners, both in terms of children and teachers. However, the learning for teachers also has to lead to the improvement and development of their practice. Crucial to the learning within a community of practice is that the individuals participate in the activities of the community together. The teachers within the thinking school are working towards a common vision and purpose and learn through informal integration in the workplace while also learning collaboratively through formally designed activities for learning.

Building a dynamic learning community

My research sought to identify the complex factors that influence teachers' learning experiences in primary schools. I evaluated teachers' perceptions of these factors and drew on them to build a model for the provision of positive formal and informal learning for teachers in primary schools. This book is about how to introduce and develop this model within your own schools.

Key features of this model include specific teacher learning activities that can be implemented in schools to support formal learning opportunities and encourage informal learning activities within the wider development of a positive and expansive learning environment.

To enable this model to work successfully, it is imperative that teacher learning is led by learning-focused leaders who are able to work in partnership with teachers and contribute to the learning activities. Learning-focused leaders judge everything they do in terms of its impact on children's and adults' learning. Through engagement in a dynamic community of learners, teachers in turn develop the skills of learning-focused leadership. The community itself then continues to innovate, grow and develop. I describe the learning community in the model as dynamic because my work has shown that the development of these key learning activities has a dynamic effect on teacher learning in schools. The structures within the model create a culture within the school that in turn promotes the development of positive attitudes to learning.

All members of staff will become and develop the skills of learning-focused leaders. The model uses the word 'dynamic' to define both the system within the learning community 'characterised by constant change and progress' and the learning-focused leaders who are 'positive in attitude and full of energy and new ideas'. I have designed a model that I hope will inform the future implementation of teacher learning activities in primary schools, and promote expansive, personalised formal and informal learning activities. I am passionate in my belief that if you implement this model, you will see a significant positive impact on the learning of all the children in your school.

Summary

In this first chapter, I outlined my belief that the single most important factor that influences the quality of teaching in schools is the quality of teacher learning. I discussed the potential challenges facing our profession in the UK over the next few years. I shared some of my personal experiences and explained that this book reflects both my research findings and my own practical experience of teaching and leading in primary schools over the years.

I briefly introduced workplace learning theories – in particular situated learning and communities of practice – because workplace learning theories influenced and changed my thinking on effective teacher learning. Teacher professional learning has much to gain from workplace learning, particularly in terms of creating a structure and culture in schools to maximise informal learning opportunities for teachers. Essential to the model of the thinking school are the activities of the dynamic learning community. These activities represent the findings of my research and practice and reflect the strategies that I believe need to be promoted and implemented in schools to maximise teacher professional learning. At the heart of the thinking school, all members of staff become learning-focused leaders and reflective, critical thinkers.

The key components of the thinking school are discussed in depth in each one of the following chapters.

Chapter 2. The dynamic learning community in the thinking school

This chapter outlines the key dimensions of the dynamic learning community at the heart of the thinking school and suggests how to develop the model in your own school. The formal learning activities that need implementing in the thinking school will promote informal learning across the school and build relational qualities such as informal professional dialogue and a culture of high challenge and high trust, focused on pupil learning outcomes.

Chapter 3. Leadership in the thinking school

School leaders are crucial in modelling learning behaviours and attitudes for the staff and children. Every action of the school leaders is scrutinised, and it is imperative that they lead by example, leading staff learning and leading teaching. In this chapter, we see how the attitudes and behaviours of learning-focused leaders in the thinking school promote positive dispositions to learning amongst the staff. The key is in enabling all staff and children to see themselves as lifelong learners, confident in innovating and not worried about making mistakes. School leaders set the structures and cultures that underpin the successful development of the thinking school. We see that distributed leadership ensures that all staff bring their brains to work and see themselves as authentic learning-focused leaders.

Chapter 4. Activities in the thinking school

This chapter illustrates the value of particular activities in providing powerful learning opportunities, and their potential impact on the development of individual dispositions to learning. This promotes a culture within the workplace that enables informal learning to thrive. I show how all staff will benefit from engaging in research-based practice, and how it is particularly important to enable all staff to engage in peer learning and lesson studies. The wider the range of people across the school who take part in professional dialogue of this kind, the better. Two of the most powerful pedagogical subjects are also explored: assessment for learning and talk for learning.

Chapter 5. Developing the culture in the thinking school

Implementing the structures detailed in this book won't maximise teacher learning on its own. Chapter 5 describes how a culture needs to be developed at the school that promotes collaborative learning, innovation, risk-taking, critical thinking, and professional enquiry and dialogue. Findings from my research identify the factors that affect teacher engagement in professional learning in school. Opportunities are highlighted for collaborative research and working within and across different groups in the school. Learning-focused leaders need to be open and transparent in their practice, and specifically when modelling and team-teaching. In the thinking school, all staff should be given opportunities to develop coaching skills, as coaching is designed to empower all staff to become solution focused.

Relevant reading

Cordingley, P., Higgins, S., Greany, T., Buckler, N., Coles-Jordan, D., Crisp, B., Saunders, L. and Coe, R. (2015) *Developing great teaching: lessons from the international reviews into effective professional development.* London: Teacher Development Trust.

Eurydice (2015) *The teaching profession in Europe: practices, perceptions, and policies.* Luxembourg: Publications Office of the European Union.

Hodkinson, H. and Hodkinson, P. (2005) 'Improving schoolteachers' workplace learning', *Research Papers in Education* 20 (2) pp. 109–131.

Lave, J. and Wenger, E. (1991) *Situated learning.* Cambridge: Cambridge University Press.

UCET (2011) *UCET annual report 2011: educating the UK's educators.* London: UCEL Institute of Education.

Wenger, E. (2008) *Communities of practice: a brief introduction.* Available at: www.goo.gl/SAUovq (Accessed 28th November 2018)

Reflective questions

1. What challenges do you think your school could potentially be facing in the next three years?

2. How would you describe your own professional learning experiences during your career?

3. How highly is teacher learning valued at your school?

4. How would you describe the staff learning culture at your school?

5. How would you like to see teacher learning develop or improve at your school?

6. What might be the impact of developing situated learning at your school?

Chapter 2

The dynamic learning community in the thinking school

Defining dynamic learning

I have always been confident that our most committed and reflective practitioners in school are also our most effective and I strongly believe that school leaders make a powerful difference to teachers' experiences and children's learning. However, at the beginning of my research I did not necessarily know how to go about creating such a learning community. My extensive research and experience has led me to the assertion that we can implement activities in our schools that purposefully both create expansive learning opportunities for our teachers and promote the development of a culture at the school that supports informal learning amongst staff.

My doctoral research found that the relationship between engagement in learning activities and the expansiveness of the learning environment is a dynamic process – they impact on each other. The evidence suggested that engaging in activities such as peer learning supports the development of a community of learners while also encouraging positive attitudes to learning amongst individuals. The quality of the learning environment for teachers varies widely between schools. Consequently, the quality of children's learning experience also varies. Much more can be done to improve teacher learning experiences in schools. The teachers I interviewed for my research spoke about the significance of learning that happened informally within their year group teams and across the school. It was clear that some of the teachers had experienced restrictive environments in their school, where their learning was constrained by organisational difficulties or lack of opportunities – they felt they didn't have a voice. They put this down directly to the decision-making within the school, particularly by their school leaders.

My findings showed unequivocally the influence of school leaders in determining the expansiveness of the learning environment – or lack of it – and whether learning opportunities were available to teachers. The teachers I interviewed valued opportunities for collaborative planning highly, seeing such activities as promoting a positive culture for learning within the school. They view school leaders to be in a position to design professional learning opportunities that enable them to engage in professional dialogue and learn collaboratively with and from each other. From these findings, I developed the concept of the dynamic learning community within the thinking school. At its best, it can be applied to all children and staff, enhancing the wellbeing and attainment of all. And it is applicable to all types of settings, from small primary schools to large secondaries.

School leaders need to be both confident and humble: confident because they are informed about their practice and aren't afraid to be creative and take risks; humble and accepting that they can learn from their peers. They are open and transparent in their professional dialogue with staff, maintaining the focus on children's learning and progress. They operate in a culture of high challenge and high trust, able to challenge the team to achieve optimal outcomes for their students yet open to challenge from team members because it's all about the impact of their actions on children's learning.

My research found that teachers have individual choice in the extent to which they choose to engage in the learning opportunities on offer, and their engagement is dependent on how well the activities are personalised to their own and their children's learning needs. This was clearly linked to teacher motivation and the perceived need for teachers to have professional learning opportunities that reflected their learning needs.

I spoke with teachers and listened to their reflections on how colleagues want to learn in different ways and that some colleagues were viewed as having negative attitudes to learning or a closed mind to new learning experiences. One of the key principles for the design of the dynamic learning community is to enable teachers to develop positive attitudes towards both their own individual learning and collaborative learning with colleagues.

Often when I am presenting a talk on the thinking school to senior leaders, I am asked the question: 'How do I get rid of underperforming teachers?' Considering the fact that I am usually extolling the virtues of teacher engagement in a wide and diverse range of professional learning activities, this question is disheartening. I always answer the question in the same way. If a teacher is motivated to develop and improve, then regardless of their starting points, school leaders can and should enable their professional learning and development. When I arrived at my current school, I worked with a number of teachers that had only been in the profession for two or three years. Their professional capabilities had been questioned, yet I could see that they had a personal drive and motivation to be successful. We need to remember that teachers are developing their craft during their first few years of practice, and we need to give them opportunities to learn and improve. One of those teachers has since told me that they would probably have left the profession if those negative early experiences had continued.

We have to believe that with the right culture and conditions in place, our teachers can learn and develop in the same ways that we believe children can learn and develop. We wouldn't give up on children, so why are we so quick to give up on teachers? Admittedly, there are teachers that I have worked with that have demonstrated a reluctance to improve and a lack of commitment to recognise children's learning as the core purpose of their work. However, these teachers are rare exceptions and should have no place in either your own school or the profession.

The dynamic learning community is designed to be collaborative and if you are a member of staff at the thinking school, you have to be committed to keep on learning. If this is valued and modelled continuously, my experience tells me that teachers who don't share those same values will look to move on. I will show how engagement in activities such as action research, peer learning and lesson study enable teachers to gain confidence and become more positive about their learning.

Key features of the dynamic learning community

There are key features within the dynamic learning community that we encourage to develop in the thinking school. To enable the model to work successfully, it is imperative that teacher learning is led by learning-focused leaders who are able to work in partnership with teachers and contribute to learning activities.

This dynamic learning community cultivates learning-focused leaders. Through modelling and coaching the values and skills of learning-focused leadership, participation within the dynamic learning community encourages all staff to internalise and hold these values and develop these skills. An authentic distributed leadership model will ensure that all staff see themselves as learning-focused leaders. Learning-focused leadership is essential in supporting and maximising opportunities for informal learning (Eraut, 2004).

In table 1, I have charted the key factors that the findings from my research and practice suggest will support teacher professional learning.

Formal learning activities	Informal learning outcomes
Research-based practice: Formal opportunities made available to think creatively and trial changes to practice	**Reflective practitioners:** Reflective practice is seen by teachers as part of their role – they question their practice and take risks
Teacher choice in learning: Opportunities for teachers to select their own focus for professional learning, matched to their individual learning needs	**Personal drive to learn:** Teachers are highly motivated and they develop a personal drive for their continual learning
Learning relating to children: Relating teacher learning to children's learning needs and their day-to-day practice	**Staff focus on children's learning:** Professional learning and dialogue between staff will focus directly on children's learning and practice

Formal learning activities	Informal learning outcomes
Coaching opportunities for all staff: Every staff member trained in coaching, and given opportunities to coach and be coached	**High challenge and high trust:** Staff feel valued and privileged to work in a culture of high trust and high challenge. They are solution focused
Formal collaborative learning: Formal opportunities that support collaborative learning: collaborative planning; opportunities to work in different groups; peer learning and lesson study; modelling of practice	**Informal collaborative learning:** Activities that then support informal collaborative learning through professional dialogue amongst staff. Learning-focused leaders model learning behaviours and mindsets
Time for formal learning: Time made available for formal learning opportunities as part of role of teacher, e.g. to conduct research	**Time for informal learning:** Time made available for informal learning opportunities, e.g. collaborative planning
Non-judgemental learning evaluations: Lesson observations focused on professional collaborative learning	**Learning evaluations are informal and trusting:** Evaluations of teaching and learning take place informally in a safe, supportive and collaborative learning environment
Intellectually challenging learning opportunities: Learning activities that are personalised and challenging, with the aim of encouraging intellectual creativity and curiosity	**Teachers value learning:** Workplace is seen as a place where staff learning is as important as children's learning

Table 1: The Dynamic Learning Community

In the thinking school, I am arguing that through the effective implementation of the eight formal learning activities, there will be an associated dynamic effect in supporting the development of informal learning across the school. These informal learning activities will then impact upon teachers' attitudes to their own and others' learning within the school. I accept that the development of this learning community is not straightforward. It's not simply a case of setting up these formal activities and expecting this expansive learning environment of individuals with positive dispositions to learning to magically appear. School leaders need to lead by example and develop a learning environment over time that ensures that teachers' and children's learning is at the centre of all activities at the school. Effective teacher learning is linked to effective leadership, and it is important that teacher learning activities are not seen as something additional to do.

A consistent implementation of these activities will ensure that the learning environment supports the development of teacher learning through formal and informal workplace learning activities. These activities will have a positive impact on teacher wellbeing and individual dispositions to learning and in turn support the development of learning-focused leaders. The central premise of the thinking school is that we are developing a community of learners who are evaluating their practice in an ongoing cycle of improvement. I am not saying that schools cannot be successful if they don't work in the ways that I've described. I'm arguing that by becoming a thinking school, they can become even more successful.

We have to ensure that we channel our resources effectively; and in the thinking school, we prioritise teacher learning activities because we understand the significant power that they hold in enabling our children's learning. This is why time is allocated during the day to specific collaborative learning activities that we value, including collaborative planning, peer learning, lesson study and action research. In the thinking school, we know that action research has the potential to provide more time for teacher learning and a potentially more personally relevant and meaningful learning experience.

The dynamic learning community is at the centre of the thinking school, and we can judge the effectiveness of the learning community by measuring its impact on new entrants to the workplace. This might be a student teacher or NQT but it is important to evaluate the relative impact on the NQT upon joining the thinking school. Taking the example of three NQTs that joined our school one year, I can assess the dynamic learning community model and its impact on each of them. All three of them had been student teachers with us and turned down job offers at other schools to join us. They were therefore motivated to join us because of their experiences as student teachers – this is clearly linked to the successful recruitment of teachers.

They joined an established thinking school, and experienced all the expansive learning opportunities made available to them. They started in September 2015 and have each: completed a successful induction year; either completed their MA or are on their way to completing it; mentored student teachers themselves; taken on leadership responsibilities in the school; presented to student teachers at university conferences. I am confident that each of them has the potential to be leading thinking schools of their own in the future. We work with student teachers every year, and I do not have enough positions available each year to accommodate as many NQTs as would like to join us. Our job is to develop them for our profession, and I am always humbled by the positive experiences they share about their teaching practices at our school. This is a reflection of the efforts of our teachers as mentors and learning-focused leaders.

In the same way that schools are measured for the value that they have added to children's learning over time, we can do the same for teachers' learning and development. The dynamic learning community is designed to ensure that the NQT has a continuously positive learning experience at the school. I believe that through engagement in the learning community, a teacher's learning and development will be accelerated in comparison to the average school.

I also believe that there are teachers in our school who might have been lost to the profession if they had started as NQTs in another school with a less expansive learning environment. By engaging in the dynamic learning community, each NQT will in turn themselves become a learning-focused leader at the school. The dynamic learning community is ultimately in place to enable the professional learning of all staff, to promote their wellbeing and retain our excellent staff in the profession. That is why I firmly believe that the philosophies behind the thinking school should be shared more widely across our profession. This will impact positively on teachers' wellbeing and their retention, as well as ensuring that we are working towards a truly world-class education system for our children. Although teacher learning is seen as a key priority in impacting upon standards of teaching and pupil achievement, research continues to demonstrate that there remains a lack of access for teachers in English schools to high-quality learning activities that impact positively on their practice and pupil learning outcomes (Cordingley et al., 2015).

In the thinking school, learning activities are introduced simultaneously in order to develop teacher skills, knowledge, understanding and self-confidence, and each activity is to be implemented well in order to maximise teacher learning. Collectively, they have the potential to provide a highly expansive learning environment for all teachers and children to continually develop and accelerate their learning. The thinking school aims to develop motivated, curious, restless, intelligent, independent and articulate learners.

Research-based practice ➔ Reflective practitioners

In the thinking school, all teachers are engaged in research; sometimes individually, but mostly collaboratively. They investigate their own and each other's practice in the quest for continual improvement. The learning environment encourages engagement in research, and provides resources for teachers to undertake it effectively. Teachers can access research from across the world that promotes thinking and reflection upon practice. Strong partnerships with leading universities ensure that, as teachers begin to specialise in their research, they can access researchers and tutors who develop their thinking.

We encourage teachers to seek academic accreditation for their research or share their findings beyond our school. Their regular engagement in collaborative action research influences the children's attainment. Teachers use their research findings to inform practice across the school, so it is evidence-based. Regular engagement in research makes for informed reflective practitioners who constantly develop and improve their practice.

This makes teachers receptive to informal learning within the workplace. Trialling and evaluating changes to their practice becomes a habit. We call it creativity through successive failures. They are curious and take risks in their practice to continually improve. This becomes embedded in the school's culture. Teachers question their practice and they discuss their practice. They informally share their findings and reflections, initially within their own year group teams, and then across the school.

Teachers in master's study groups develop strong working relationships as they complete writing assignments together. The groups form informal communities of learners across the school, exploring children's learning from Nursery to Year 6. They want to find out what is working well in other classrooms, and share their findings enthusiastically. The teachers in the thinking school are developing their wider professional understanding. They are interested in the world of education beyond their schools and bring ideas and reflections back to improve their practice.

Teacher choice in learning ⟶ Personal drive to learn

When teachers engage in learning activities they don't see as personally relevant to their own learning needs, they seldom persevere. For example, early years practitioners are often left exasperated with having to sit through PLMs that are more appropriate for Key Stage 2 teachers. Design your PLMs to link to whole-school learning objectives that enable groups of teachers to contextualise the learning for their particular cohorts of children. And do not underestimate the power of professional dialogue between teachers from different areas of the school. What came through clearly from the research was that teachers were more motivated to engage in their learning when they were given some choice in what they learned about. This depended on the relevance to their present job and also where they were in their own professional development. Teachers want to have a voice and to drive their own learning.

Action research enables teachers to identify the topics they want to explore and the key research questions to focus on. Critics may argue that increased teacher choice will result in incoherence and lack of focus. I think it will do the opposite, if you ensure that all of our collective work is focused on improving children's learning outcomes. Remember we want our teachers to bring their brains to work. It is the difference between a learner being told a theory, and discovering that theory for themselves. We are more likely to retain learning if we have been able to discover it for ourselves. When I first asked every teacher to engage in collaborative action research, the whole-school topic was assessment for learning. However, within this overarching topic, each teacher had the opportunity to explore a particular aspect of AfL. I wanted each team to choose something that they were interested in finding out more about – their findings would be their own discovery, and more likely to influence their practice.

I deliberately give responsibility back to each teacher to drive their own professional learning and development. They have to demonstrate their commitment and knowledge about areas of their practice that they need to develop, and the school leaders' responsibility is to provide the environment, tools and resources to enable them to learn. If all teachers receive coaching, their professional learning is personalised to their own needs. The individual areas for development can be targeted and met at the same time as whole-school areas for development.

The informal impact of this teacher choice is that we develop practitioners who are self-motivated and independent learners. They have a personal drive for their continual learning, so teachers' learning is not taking place only during formal meetings designated for their professional development. Teachers are determined and focused because they know their learning can benefit the children they work with. They are engaged because they want to share their practice with their team and the school. They are not engaged in professional learning that is being done 'to' them; they are driving their own learning, eager to continually improve. They come to expect and demand that school leaders give them support and expansive opportunities to continue to keep developing.

Learning related to children ➔ Staff focus on children's learning

The teachers' passion and energy for their professional learning are directed at their children's learning. Unfortunately, I have seen too many generic professional learning activities that either aren't personalised to individual teachers or aren't sufficiently related to children's learning needs. My research found that the teachers were motivated to engage in professional learning that directly related to their current practice. Every class is different, so our analysis should be focused on practice and the individual learning needs of the children in the class and how to help them learn and develop.

Teaching can be a challenging and stressful job so we need to know that our learning will improve our day-to-day practice. The activities within the dynamic learning community are designed to enable learning over time, but their flexibility allows the teachers to make immediate changes to their practice. Collaborating with others allows teachers to discuss their children's learning. My research strongly suggested that a focus on their current practice effectively motivated the teachers to carry out relevant research.

Because the children's learning is at the centre of our collective discussions and collective focus, collaborative planning sessions will focus on children they are teaching, particularly those who are not progressing well. If there are any such children, the quality of the challenge in the classroom will be examined to see whether it enables the children to make accelerated progress. Teacher learning is targeted at children's outcomes and their development. The children's learning is seen as the collective responsibility of the staff, thus involving teachers who have taught the children in previous years. We draw on the knowledge and experiences of others when supporting our children's learning.

Coaching opportunities for all staff → High challenge and high trust

The opportunity to be coached has been a fantastic professional learning experience for me. I believe that every member of staff at the thinking school should be trained in coaching, and should coach and be coached regularly. Teachers who have developed coaching skills and expertise put them to good use in informal interactions with colleagues. Team leaders and learning leaders (phase leaders) at my school are expected to participate in coaching sessions once a fortnight and to use their coaching skills to develop their team.

Coaching can be seen as the glue that binds together the learning community. Teachers can present the key challenges they face in their current role and be coached to reflect on them so they arrive at key actions that will work towards a solution. As they develop their self-reflection and evaluation skills, they begin analysing their practice deeply, thinking proactively and creatively. A whole-school commitment to coaching that is continuous is needed in order for it to be optimally effective to staff learning and school improvement, and promote informal learning.

The purpose of coaching is for staff to become more solution-focused, but it also sends out a message that we have responsibility for each other's professional learning. Coaching is totally different from hierarchical models of professional development, depending as it does on relationships based on mutual trust in a culture of high challenge. Because we trust each other, we can have honest authentic conversations. We need to be able to tell our coach exactly what may be bothering us and what we would like to develop in our practice. Coaching encourages staff to be proactive and focus on their own actions and possible solutions rather than on problems and challenges. When we are coaching each other, we are showing how much we value and wish to support each other.

Formal collaborative learning ➜ Informal collaborative learning

By designing as many formal opportunities as possible for collaborative learning, we create a culture in the school that promotes informal collaborative learning opportunities. It is essential that teachers engage in collaborative learning beyond their own year group and across the school. Put simply, the more opportunities we have to work with our colleagues, the more likely we are to build a relationship with them – and we are then more likely to speak to them informally for instruction or advice. When we first enabled teachers to engage in formal collaborative learning, we did focus on year group teams. This was easier because, in one sense, the team was already established. It was also more straightforward to plan for these opportunities. As the learning community grows and develops, we actively go beyond year group teams. This engagement in learning with a wider range of people encourages teachers to engage in informal collaborative learning and professional dialogue across the school. This is fundamental in the development of the dynamic learning community and the building of trust across the school.

Teachers are released together to assess, evaluate and plan collaboratively for children's learning. Teachers also get regular opportunities to engage in collaborative action research, peer learning and lesson study. These activities require a high degree of trust as teams of teachers are collectively interpreting and evaluating the learning that is taking place in each other's classrooms. It is up to leaders to ensure that these opportunities are made available to teachers. We have also moved away from individual observations of teacher learning, to evaluations of practice across year group teams. Two learning-focused leaders conduct a learning walk across the three classrooms, observing the children's learning (and that of the adults interacting with them), looking in books, and speaking to the children. Feedback takes place through a collaborative professional learning conversation with all the participants present, where observers, teachers and teaching assistants are able to discuss, interpret and share their experiences. This modelling and sharing of practice then proceeds across the school, and teachers organise their own learning walks, peer learning and team-teaching sessions.

It is therefore not about an evaluation or critical assessment of each individual teacher, but an assessment of the effectiveness of the team in enabling all children to learn and progress. We believe that there is a strong associated impact on teachers' engagement in informal professional dialogue across the school. These activities are designed to build trust within and beyond year group teams across the school. The activities I have highlighted promote the development of positive individual dispositions to learning and can potentially serve to even out the differences in teacher attitudes to learning across the school.

During my presentation at a recent conference, I explained what I believe to be the value of engagement in collaborative professional learning activities and its associated impact on teachers' engagement in informal professional dialogue. One participant, a senior leader in a school, wanted to know why I was making teachers talk about children's learning during their lunchtimes and breaks! I explained that I didn't make teachers do it and that teachers were choosing to engage in it because they had a motivation for their work and were interested in their children's learning and progress. It is a natural by-product of the development of the dynamic learning community in the thinking school, but I don't think she was convinced at all. Learning-focused leaders model their commitment to collaborative learning and to finding solutions collectively as a team.

Time for formal learning ⟶ Time for informal learning

During my research, I found that there was a resonance amongst teachers about perceived frustrations regarding their professional learning experiences. Time was a recurring theme.

Firstly, teachers felt that they were already overworked and committed to regular additional hours of work both at school and at home. So even if they were motivated to engage in professional learning, they felt they didn't have the time and energy to do so. For example, teachers were reluctant to engage in research because they didn't see where they were going to find the time to do it. Many professional learning activities were seen by teachers to be imposing unnecessary additional duties in a very crowded and heavy working week.

The second major aspect of time was that teachers were keen to engage in learning over time but this did not reflect their traditional experiences of professional learning at their schools. Too often, their CPL programmes in schools were dominated by one-off sessions on different topics, rather than exploring a topic in depth. (Teachers were likely to view one-day off-site courses as positive learning experiences, but I suspect that this perceived value was more often due to the fact that it was a day out of school than it was due to the courses' impact on children's learning.) Fewer opportunities were given to develop a deeper understanding of a topic over an extended period of time.

As leaders in schools, therefore, we have to do our best to ensure that teachers are given the time to engage in quality professional learning activities as well as engagement in learning activities over time. I am aware that the argument will be presented that budget cuts and limited resources will make it even more challenging to provide teachers with learning opportunities during the school day. However, I think it is equally worth acknowledging the potential benefits of investing in our teachers' learning. This investment of time and resources will impact on teachers' engagement in their own learning in a positive way, and the entire purpose of teacher learning is to enable us to improve children's learning and outcomes. We have to invest in our teachers' learning if we want our children to be as successful as possible. Teachers engage in learning during the day when they have the energy to learn more deeply, as opposed to in a meeting after school when they are more likely to be tired. Although teachers are away from their own classes for this time, their learning will benefit their children even more over time.

I also believe that it will promote teachers' wellbeing and that this will impact positively on the school budget through less teacher absence, as well as the successful recruitment and retention of staff. Teacher engagement in collaborative learning, action research, peer learning, lesson study, team-teaching, participating in and leading networks, modelling and coaching – these all take place during the school day. These activities all include formal learning opportunities for teachers during the school day that will in turn encourage teacher engagement in informal learning and professional dialogue beyond the school day. We are demonstrating the value of teacher learning by giving them time to learn and reflect during the school day.

Non-judgemental learning evaluations → Learning evaluations are informal and trusting

There remains too great a focus in schools on lesson observations that are used to judge teachers. Once a practitioner knows that they are being observed for such a purpose, they play safe and avoid risks, so the observation has little value as a learning experience. School leaders have to evaluate and provide evidence of the impact of teachers on children's learning but to do so requires far more than a single lesson observation. To evaluate the quality of our teachers in impacting upon our children's learning, we draw upon a range of evidence and we include this evidence in teacher profiles that we have created. Some of these profiles contain over six years of evidence, including: evaluations of teaching; pupil progress data; parent voice; pupil voice; learning walks; evidence in books; master's assignments; teacher reflections; evaluations of planning. This evidence is also used to inform appraisals, to validate our teachers' successes and to document the development in their professional learning.

This enables us to ensure that our lesson observations are powerful learning opportunities for our teachers. We are not using them to provide judgements of our teachers; instead we are using them as a starting point for our professional dialogue. We value teachers taking creative risks during these lesson observations because we believe that more potential learning can therefore take place. Increasingly, these learning conversations now take place between entire teams of teachers to ensure that we all have opportunities to learn from each other. This is a deliberate move away from the traditional model of a single senior leader observing and providing individual feedback. I particularly value the opportunity to go into classrooms to see the rich and diverse practice that is taking place across the school. We can all learn from each other within this culture of collaborative learning in the thinking school. Teachers actively and routinely ask me to come in and analyse aspects of their practice that they may have been working on and developing. In fact, I think they would be disappointed if I didn't come in to see their teaching and engage in a professional learning conversation with them.

The fact that lesson observations aren't judgemental means that teachers are much more comfortable in opening up and discussing their own and each other's practice. Rather than seeing themselves in competition with their colleagues, they are more likely to actively seek out their colleagues' opinions. Informal learning evaluations take place where teachers organise opportunities to visit each other's classrooms or to team-teach. Learning evaluations move away from the traditional monitoring exercise to a learning activity. Teachers develop a hunger to keep improving so they seek out opportunities to observe each other's teaching, planning, marking and assessments. The negative legacy of judgemental lesson observations is such that seeing non-judgemental ones as an expansive learning opportunity can take a lot longer for experienced staff than those new to the profession and to the thinking school.

Intellectually challenging learning opportunities ➔ Teachers value learning

We want all our children to be intellectually creative and curious, with a passion and thirst for continual lifelong learning – and should want our teachers to develop in the same way. The aim of the thinking school is to create an expansive learning environment in which all members of the dynamic learning community see themselves as learners. Whether it's children or adults, the learning activities we present them with need to be intellectually challenging. Activities that are too easy or too hard are inherently demotivating. We need learning activities that start from where the learner is currently, and challenge their thinking to move them on. During my research, teachers discussed the perceived value of learning activities that were personalised to their learning but also intellectually challenging. They felt that they had done many of the activities before, or that the activities weren't relevant to them, weren't intellectually challenging or didn't present any new theories and ideas.

We want our teachers to value their own professional learning and to know that teacher professional learning is as highly valued as – and pivotal to – children's learning. We want to give teachers research articles that challenge their thinking. We want teachers to be open to new theories and ideas, and to re-engage with those that ignited their thinking during earlier study. We want teachers to challenge each other's thinking through critical professional dialogue in a trusting learning environment, and we want to provide learning activities that excite teachers and maintain their passion for teaching and learning. By giving teachers intellectually challenging learning activities, we demonstrate how much we value their learning. The teachers grow and develop as practitioners. Informally, they may engage in intellectually challenging activities beyond the school – for example, exploring data or reading about educational theory and proven good practice. Most importantly, they will feel valued and value their own professional learning – and they will be motivated to go on learning. I have seen teachers' attitudes towards their own learning transform. One teacher described how she didn't feel challenged in her role – within five years she has completed an MA and has begun her professional doctorate. Another regularly engages in wider informal reading about education and is currently transforming practices for data and assessment across the school.

Summary

This chapter introduced the model of the dynamic learning community and presented the formal activities that are central to the development of a thinking school. All the activities are designed to support teachers' learning and encourage their engagement in wider social learning across the school. Through their continual engagement in these activities, we create a community of learners who are committed to their own professional learning. Teachers are aware that their own learning is designed to directly impact on the children's learning.

In the following chapters, I go into further detail about how to implement these activities in your schools. The structures that we put in place in the school through these activities will directly influence the collective learning culture for staff and children.

Relevant reading

Cordingley, P., Higgins, S., Greany, T., Buckler, N., Coles-Jordan, D., Crisp, B., Saunders, L. and Coe, R. (2015) *Developing great teaching: lessons from the international reviews into effective professional development.* London: Teacher Development Trust.

Eraut, M. (2004) 'Informal learning in the workplace', *Studies in Continuing Education* 26 (2) pp. 247–273.

Reflective questions

1. How intellectually challenging are the professional learning activities at your school?

2. How much informal learning do you think takes place at your school?

3. How would a student teacher or NQT describe the learning environment at your school?

4. Which activities do you think you could easily introduce in your school?

5. What challenges might you face?

Chapter 3

Leadership
in the thinking school

Understanding situated learning and the dynamic learning community should enable you to reflect on the quality of the learning environment in the schools you work in. Schools differ in the extent to which they enable teachers to learn and develop, both formally and informally. If we accept that teachers' learning significantly impacts upon children's learning, we need to consider our learning environment and the opportunities it affords teachers to learn. This chapter considers how to develop an expansive learning environment in schools. My research findings and my own practical experience both confirm that leadership within the school is critical in the development of institutional structures and cultures that underpin a truly expansive learning environment for teachers and children. Structures represent the activities we have in place and cultures represent the attitudes to learning we have in the school.

Learning-focused leadership

I stress the need for learning-focused leadership within the school. I ensure that every member of staff, regardless of their role, sees themselves as a leader. There are two aspects of this emphasis on being learning-focused.

First, each person is focusing on their own learning and development as a practitioner. Being learning-focused means that you are constantly curious and restless about your practice, reflecting on your own planning and decision-making in light of relevant findings and research. A learning-focused leader is hungry to continually gain new knowledge and skills to be the best leader, teacher, teaching assistant, midday supervisor that they can be. Teachers engage with literature and undertake research in their own classrooms. They collaborate with colleagues within and beyond their own school; they are innovative and creative, unafraid of taking risks and making changes to their practice.

Second, learning-focused leaders are focused on the 'learning outcomes' of their children. That means that every decision is analysed in terms of an impact on children's learning – not only on academic learning and progress but also their personal, social, emotional and moral development. Example questions I receive from staff might involve re-organising the timetable, deployment of staff, purchasing of resources. I always respond by asking what the perceived impact will be on children's learning. It's a great habit to get into because it ensures that we constantly maintain our focus on the fact that our actions are directly related to improving children's learning experiences. Often, many of the decisions that are made in schools are made to suit the adults rather than the children. For example, I have always found that decisions to stream children are made because it is easier for the teachers to plan and teach, rather than for the children to learn.

In the thinking school, every member of staff sees themselves as a leader. Therefore, they need to have the opportunity to make leadership decisions and have the associated responsibilities that those decisions bring. To liberate their work, I encourage them to use the barometer of children's learning to guide their decision-making. Two examples will illustrate this.

For our annual children's Christmas lunch, we have traditionally used two halls to serve the meals to the children. This is in contrast to the single hall that we use every other day of the year. This decision had originally been made by senior leaders at the school who didn't have a background of working in school kitchens. Last Christmas, three members of the kitchen team came to see me with a plan to serve the Christmas lunch in one hall. I asked them the same question that I always ask – what will be the impact on the children? They gave me a clear rationale of how they would lead staff to ensure that there would be a positive impact on the children's lunchtime experience.

By allowing them to lead on the decision rather than forcing them to conform to a decision made on their behalf that they had never been committed to, I knew that the kitchen team would be more motivated and engaged in ensuring the success of the lunch. They were leading the learning for the children in their own area of responsibility, and they knew that I would support them to succeed. As a result, the Christmas lunch was more successful than it had ever been. The staff members in the kitchen will have developed confidence in their own decision-making. They will have developed skills that will serve them well in the future – they will consider their own roles in enabling the children to have successful lunchtime experiences. They will also be in a position in the future to be able to make leadership decisions themselves, without the need to approach a line manager for affirmation. My only role in this situation was to go to the dining hall and check in with team members to ask how it was going – as well as enjoy my Christmas lunch with the children. I had shown that I had faith in them to make effective leadership decisions in the best interests of the children.

An earlier example during my headship took place when engaging in a professional conversation with a Year 2 team leader following a maths lesson. She explained that she hadn't been happy with the children's progress during the lesson. She went on to describe how the children had been engaging brilliantly in their maths learning during the whole-class carpet session whilst using their mini-whiteboards. She then made the decision to stop the carpet session and asked them to complete questions in their maths books. She explained that she made the decision because she was worried that if the books were monitored, it would look like the children hadn't been learning any maths on that day.

As we continued the discussion, it was evident that this concern included what the potential reaction would be if I or other leaders were to look at the books. This worry was also reflective of her previous experiences of leadership. I explained to her that she had *effectively* stopped the children's learning to demonstrate to an assessor beyond the classroom that the children were learning maths! This is an example of where teachers make a decision because of the interests or demands of other adults rather than what is in the best interests of the children.

A confident learning-focused leader makes decisions that directly impact upon children's learning. I agreed with the teacher's appraisal that the children would have been better served by her spending the entire session engaging the children with whiteboard work. They should have continued talking about maths and discussing their understanding as preparation for an extended session of written work to consolidate and sharpen their skills in their books later in the week. Teachers need to be in informed charge of the decision-making for children's learning in their classrooms and year groups. Teachers make thousands of decisions every day whilst teaching, some good and some not so good. Consider what knowledge informs these decisions and the extent to which we can create an environment that enables teachers to tap into the knowledge that informs their decision-making. As leaders, we should judge the work of adults in terms of children's learning outcomes, and it is easier to do this over a period of three weeks than it is over a single lesson. The legacy of Ofsted-type single judgemental lesson observations hasn't been helpful to teachers or leaders in this regard.

Whether the leader is the headteacher, year group leader, or the kitchen leader, they should maintain a focus on the consequences of their decisions upon children's learning. As the most senior leader in the school (I discuss the value of distributed leadership later in the chapter), I have always found this emphasis on children's learning to be a powerful guiding force for each decision and every action that I take in my role. Viviane Robinson (2011) has discussed how we should evaluate leadership by its impact upon children's learning. It sounds simple and straightforward, but I think we would all benefit from considering the extent to which we do this. From my own experience, a considerable amount of time is expended in schools to explain children's underachievement. The quality of leadership should be judged, plainly and simply, through an evaluation of children's learning experiences and outcomes.

In addition, Robinson's (2011) research demonstrated that the single greatest effect of leaders on children's outcomes was the leadership of teacher learning and development. The big message coming through both from her research and from my own findings is that leadership is significant in impacting upon children's learning outcomes, and the greatest influence of leaders can be seen through their work in promoting and leading teacher learning. Consider the proportion of time that is spent at your school by leaders engaging directly with teacher learning and development. Take for example a single teacher of 30 children at my school. I cannot directly teach his 30 children each day, yet I am ultimately responsible for their learning and progress. The best way for me to support that teacher to succeed is to support his professional learning.

My message at this point to you is to ensure that every worker, as a learning-focused leader, maintains a focus on everything that they do in the workplace in terms of its impact upon children's learning. The reason I am emphasising this point is because it is easy for us in schools to get distracted from this simple aim, and it keeps us humble and grounded. On any given day in school, we may have to undertake planning, assessments, professional conversations with colleagues, parents and advisers. Consider each of these activities and the extent to which we use them to learn – both as professionals ourselves and about children's learning. Children and teacher learning must be at the centre of everything that we do, and it's worthwhile for us to consider all the factors that potentially distract us from maintaining that focus.

Values-led leadership

Values inform our actions in the workplace. Consider your core values and how these influence your decision-making. It is not as simple as just saying that we evaluate each decision in terms of its impact upon children's learning. This means nothing if we don't hold high expectations for all and genuinely believe that every child can achieve. There is the tendency for schools to have a fixed mindset about children's learning and their potential achievements. It is common practice for us to group children according to their current attainment and we routinely label children as high ability or low ability. I never use these phrases and instead use the terms lower or higher attaining according to their current attainment. 'Ability' implies that the pecking order in the classroom will be maintained as the children grow. Focus instead on effort and emphasise the fact that effort (rather than ability) underpins our learning and leads to success.

When I have learning conversations with children, they are able to articulate who is the best mathematician or artist in their class and often they assume that this is because of some inherited ability – 'He is just cleverer than me'. What I have to repeat to children is that they are not competing with each other but they are competing with themselves. I use the higher-attaining child to demonstrate what learning skills they may have that the other children could equally develop – for example, resilience. Children do not necessarily display these attitudes regarding fixed ability in other aspects of their life. For example, they know that if they independently keep playing a computer game, they will get better and better at it; do they feel this way when they approach a page of sums or a piece of writing, or are they reliant on guidance from the teacher? Once you have a child that believes perseverance brings success, you have developed a learner.

Consider the extent to which your learning environment promotes this mentality. We would never dare to group our teachers in a PLM according to their ability or current attainment. Why not? Because it would not be good for their self-esteem. So why do it for children? Grouping children by ability in a classroom can serve to widen the gap in attainment.

As every teacher in our school teaches, regardless of their leadership position, we are able to teach our children in smaller groups for core subjects where appropriate. We try to have a fourth experienced teacher available for at least three mornings a week in each year group. It is up to the team to decide how this additional lead teacher is deployed, according to the needs of the children. It may mean that children across the year group are split into four groups. Or it could be that focus groups of children are removed from the classroom for specific interventions, allowing the class teacher to teach a smaller group. We can afford this because we have a smaller senior leadership team.

In Year 6, my deputy and I both teach for approximately 40% of the week. This enables us to group our 90 children into five smaller groups. Children are not necessarily grouped according to their current attainment but more in line with their learning needs. I will often work with the children who may have additional language or personal and social needs. We also lead an additional reading group for select children across the three classes, giving the teachers a smaller class to work with. The children work in an environment designed to develop their metacognitive skills and self-esteem as learners. Our learning-focused leadership secures positive outcomes for our children. In 2017, out of 762 schools of a similar size in England, we were the eighth-highest-performing school for maths attainment at Key Stage 2. We were also the highest-performing school in the local authority for children's progress across reading, writing and maths. Values-led leadership keeps us grounded and humble, and enables us to accept that as adults we are always learning, and that there are no limits to children's learning and progress.

In the most successful schools, all staff share a strong moral purpose and vision for children's learning, and the vision is underpinned by core values. This also relates to shared expectations for teacher learning. This central vision is not imposed from above by school leaders, but is co-constructed based on our common core values. This is central to our work, where every voice is heard and listened to. As every member of staff is learning, they are better able to adapt to the context in which they are working, and transform according to children's needs. We have to accept that we are working in an environment in which we experience continual change, both at a macro level in terms of national initiatives and a micro level in terms of the children we teach. We therefore need to develop the skills to positively manage these changes as a central tenet of our core vision. A barometer for evaluating the strength of this core vision is to ask five different people within the school the same question and evaluate the continuity of the responses.

Involve all your teachers in school leadership decisions. I am not advocating holding a referendum for every decision, but ensure that all staff have a voice and the opportunity to inform decision-making.

It is demotivating for teachers to be asked to do something without understanding why. Teachers spend significant amounts of time in marking children's work and will usually follow a strict marking and feedback policy. Often, this marking is undertaken for monitoring purposes by leaders rather than for its direct pedagogical impact upon children's learning.

All staff should be involved in the development of such policies and this will support their motivation and confidence in understanding and adhering to the policies. We spent two years revising our school policy on feedback. The policy was informed by all teachers, following their engagement in theory, research in their classrooms, visits to other schools, and extensive professional dialogue. Two of the teachers that led our development work on feedback have since been involved in research-informed peer reviews across several schools, with a specific focus on enabling teachers to develop their knowledge and practice of effective feedback to children.

In too many schools, leaders make decisions and expect every teacher to conform without question. Any sign of challenge or questioning would be frowned upon by leaders – I actively encourage all staff to question and challenge (where appropriate) any of our policies and actions, in the best interests of our children. When I first arrived at my current school, I was told never to go back on a decision I or any other leader had made, as it could either be undermining or denote weak leadership. I suggest the opposite: it is a sign of strength when you change your decision (even reversing it) if doing so is in the best interests of the children.

What does values-led leadership look like in practice? Every decision you make and every action you take as a leader in a school is scrutinised. These actions and decisions reflect your values. My staff know that I care about the children and they see this in the way I speak to them and about them. The children in our school know how much I enjoy being with them and working with them and they see this in my daily actions. When publicly questioned about the impact of my leadership, one teacher at my school clarified that she perceived my greatest influence was felt through the way in which I directly worked and interacted with the children. You are modelling to your team how you expect them to lead, for example how you want your staff to talk to children. The way in which you nurture and care for the learning and wellbeing of your staff is exactly how you want your staff to treat the children and each other, and how you hope the children will treat each other. This is the basis of building trust in the workplace. The extent to which leader and staff behaviour is authentic, consistent and grounded in respect for all staff, children and parents has a big impact on the emotional and learning climate within the school.

If we share our meaningful goals within the workplace, we share a worthwhile purpose. I constantly talk about the importance of children's personal development as well as their academic development. I will say to children and adults that there's no value in being a good mathematician or writer if you are not also a good person. We want children to develop positive values and make a positive contribution to society. We have a relentless drive and focus on the personal, social, emotional and academic development of our children, and this informs all our decision-making and evaluations. We believe in the value of reflection and learning for all within the organisation so that everyone strives to learn, develop and improve their practice and outcomes.

Consistency matters and a leader only has to slip once to lose people's trust. You may continually send a message that children and staff need to be valued, nurtured and developed, but you would only need to be seen shouting at one child or upsetting one member of staff to lose people's trust and your own credibility. Your actions will be consistent only if they are informed by your core values and beliefs. A person's self-esteem and view of themselves as a learner impact upon their engagement in and experiences of learning. This belief influences my actions, and my interactions with staff and children are designed to build their self-esteem as learners. I praise the efforts of staff and children because I believe that effort leads to success. It's a case of catching people doing things right. It could be a display you particularly like, an assembly you particularly enjoyed, or sharing with staff positive comments from the children they are teaching. I write to each member of staff at the end of each term and I detail certain things that I may have noticed about their development and growth as practitioners.

The challenge in the thinking school is to take the vision and values to deeper levels. Invite the staff at your school to share what they believe to be the qualities of a good person and even a good community. Are these values shared within the learning community across the school? Learning-focused leaders publicly demonstrate their values in what they say and what they do. In the classroom, children will internalise the values that their teacher holds. If the teacher is constantly and consistently demonstrating the importance of every child having a voice, and learning from mistakes, the children will also learn these values. It sounds simple. The children I teach constantly tell me when they don't understand something, and will repeat publicly the value of identifying and learning from mistakes. As a leader, you should not expect your staff to undertake any actions or behaviours that you would not equally be prepared to undertake. You lead by example and are aware that you are continually modelling and articulating the beliefs and values you hold about learning – both for children and staff.

Values-led leadership will support you in retaining your best staff. When a teacher praises a child in their class, they are demonstrating to the rest of the class the qualities and skills they value. Equally, when you praise a member of your team, you articulate to all staff what you value. I will value effort and examples of staff demonstrating their care for the children and publicly detail how their work has impacted positively on children's learning. I also value examples of staff developing their own learning and working collaboratively with others. As with children, the praise is always evaluative. I will detail what the person has done and how it has made a difference to our children and our school. I don't give out false praise because it doesn't support learning and growth.

I have seen schools where people are promoted because of the fact that they are forceful and seek to control team members through coercion. This type of leader is not learning-focused and will not enable as much learning of staff and children as would be possible otherwise. We can be encouraging of learning and make sure our children and staff have a wonderful day at school. We can ensure they take risks with their learning and continually grow and develop. Equally, our actions as leaders can make our children and staff anxious, nervous or even frustrated and angry. Our job is to create a positive learning environment for all. Too many leaders don't want to authentically distribute responsibility to their team members. They feel that they have to tell people what to do, to control them and monitor them. This does not support a culture of trust and self-reflection and development.

I recall one teacher during my first year of headship making a particularly negative comment about a child in her class, implying a fixed mindset about his capabilities. I knew from that one moment that she would not be able to be a leader within our school, unless that mindset changed. I knew that the child would not make the progress that he was capable of in this class because the teacher did not believe he could. It is difficult for people to change if they are not prepared to examine their core values. By sharing our values, we will grow leaders that reflect those same values. When you promote or recruit a member of staff, you send a powerful message to the rest of the team about the kind of qualities you value in a person working at your school.

I have worked with leaders who insist on being in control and telling people what to do, and monitoring the extent to which they do it. During my second year of headship, some of these more forceful leaders began to look to leave the school. It is so important to be honest with your staff. One of our leaders could be both patronising and intimidating in her leadership of colleagues. I had a discussion with her and asked her if she realised that staff members found her behaviour intimidating. She seemed shocked by what I had said – her shock was more to do with the fact that no one had ever dared to tell her this before. Her leadership was leading to poor outcomes for our children, so I had no hesitation in telling her this. During that period, I deliberately hired two experienced team leaders who had strong emotional literacy skills and a commitment to more collaborative working and leadership. This had a positive impact on both the emotional climate of the school and the learning and development of team members.

If your staff and children share a strong sense of core values, they behave in a way which supports good learning for all. We are a Unicef Rights Respecting School and have been since I started my headship. One core outcome is that the staff and children have a shared language when it comes to the behaviour and rights of all in our learning community. I provide an environment that gives all staff a voice and the opportunity to co-construct knowledge. Children do not behave in a particular way because the teacher has told them to and teachers do not behave in a particular way because the headteacher has told them to. Teachers do something because it is the right thing to do.

Consider the extent to which the actions of staff at your school reflect their espoused values – to what extent do we do what we actually say we do, and how well do these actions reflect our values? Giving everyone a voice, to express both positive and negative viewpoints, helps to build trust within the workplace. When you embed high trust within the culture and fabric of the school, it will serve to liberate people to: share their areas for development; be creative and take risks; learn and grow; and enable others around them to learn and grow.

Build an environment in which there is both high challenge and high trust. The more we trust each other, the more we are able to open up our practice and the more we are able to challenge each other. The difficulty with many teams in schools is the lack of open challenge. People feel that they cannot challenge because it will be taken personally or negatively. Challenge is accepted if the team members share common values and goals. In my first year of headship, one strategy I wanted to introduce was initially viewed by staff with suspicion. I met with team leaders to explain that I wanted each teacher to send each child's English or maths book home, accompanied with a dialogue sheet designed to engage the parents in a learning conversation with their children. My rationale was that children would really value an opportunity to share their learning at home, and that it would support parental engagement.

I was given every excuse under the sun as to why it would be a bad idea, including: 'Why bother? The parents wouldn't complete the sheet!'; 'The books would never come back!'; 'Parents would question the quality of the work, marking or teaching!'; and even that the parents were illiterate! I won't go through all my responses but I will share my response to the potential criticism from parents of children's work and marking. If the quality of the children's learning and teacher marking isn't good enough for parents, then it shouldn't be good enough for us. Alternatively, if it is unwarranted criticism, we should value the opportunity to engage with parents to share our views. On meeting with team leaders, I made sure that I listened to all the views and fears shared. I explained that I thought it was a good idea and would accept it if I was proved wrong. I asked them to commit wholeheartedly to having a trial of the process, and that we would collectively evaluate the process. If everybody didn't want to continue with it, we would stop.

This conversation was positive because it removed the potential discord. We were all committed to engaging authentically in the process and evaluating its relative success. And I clearly demonstrated my values:

- I implemented a strategy that valued parental voice and engagement in their children's learning.
- I wanted to develop a stronger learning partnership between the school and the home.
- I discussed the need to value our children's learning by having the highest expectations for standards in our books.
- I demonstrated that I was prepared to be innovative and creative and to take risks.
- The fact that I had already discussed it with two key leaders responsible for inclusion and parental engagement (and they were in full agreement) demonstrated my commitment to working in collaboration.
- I showed that I genuinely valued staff voice and would be prepared to revise my opinion if necessary.
- I also hoped to be demonstrating learning-focused leadership of staff and children.

The result, through the leadership of teachers, was a huge success – with an average return in each class of over 90% of the dialogue sheets – and it was an activity that set the standard for our future work and success. Five years later, we continue to send the books home once each term. This example demonstrates how challenge can be accepted and serve to build trust. Put simply, children's learning is at the centre, underpinned by teacher learning. Our values reflect this and inform our actions.

Developing an expansive learning environment

The key is to ensure that the formal learning opportunities made available in your school also promote informal learning. As seen in chapter 2, if formal learning activities are designed well, they will also encourage teachers to engage in informal professional learning conversations with staff members across the school. However, you can't simply put three teachers in a year group together in a room to plan and expect a fantastic learning experience for all. It doesn't work like that. Some teachers naturally seem to work brilliantly together, and others are very much the opposite. I have always ensured that teachers have preparation, planning and assessment (PPA) release time together. We use the abbreviation LRC for PPA to denote 'learning review conversations'. Some teams will use the time to have excellent learning conversations where they think collaboratively and creatively about their planning for children. Other teams are characterised by participants hidden behind their laptops, writing their own plans for individual subject areas. Learning environments in schools differ and can be more or less expansive in supporting teacher learning. Individual schools, and school leaders in particular, make decisions that influence the quality of the learning environments for teachers.

Researchers (Evans et al., 2006; Billett, 2006) have discussed the individuality of school learning environments and the extent to which the hidden workplace curriculum impacts upon the richness of learning that occurs outside more formal conceptions of learning opportunities. In their review of the impact of informal learning at work, Fuller et al. (2005) detailed how the workplace offers opportunities for workers to learn alongside colleagues and through the undertaking of their roles. This relates to Lave and Wenger's (1991) work and I found that the quality of working relationships in the school makes a significant difference to the quality of teacher learning. It is not the people within a school that make the difference to its effectiveness, but the relationships between the people that matter most. By 'relationship', I mean the quality of those working relationships and the subsequent focus upon pupil learning.

Where there is a high degree of collaboration and mutual support between colleagues, this is an influential factor in promoting learning opportunities for those workers through such informal activities as advice or occasional instruction. Learning is seen to be an integral and often unconscious part of their lives. We build this in a school by purposefully creating an environment that supports this type of learning. Returning to the example of LRC, we define clearly for the team what we expect from this formal collaborative professional learning activity and why we expect it. For the three teachers in each year group, plus support staff, student teachers and learning leaders, the time is to be used in dialogue about the learning of the 90 children. Specifically, exactly where each of the children currently is in their learning and what can be planned collaboratively to take account of where they are and challenge them to continue to learn and improve through creative and motivating learning activities. This type of professional learning will encourage informal learning as teachers will continue to discuss the children's learning experiences informally beyond their allotted LRC time because they develop a shared understanding, commitment and interest. Even where there are schools with only two or three teachers, collaboration is vital both across the school and (where possible) beyond, in partnership with other schools.

In many contexts for many workers, the informal support of a colleague can be more helpful to learning than the support of formally designated mentors. Teacher confidence comes from taking risks, meeting challenges, and feeling valued, and these experiences will only develop if the environment encourages and values mutual support and collaboration. Design your collaborative planning to enable the development of this environment. Activities such as peer learning and lesson studies will enhance this collaborative learning further.

Higher-achieving schools have a greater capacity to support teacher professional learning because of a greater emphasis on the development of conditions that promote social capital, such as trust, opportunities for collaboration, and networking. Returning to Hodkinson and Hodkinson 2005 study, their evaluation showed that collaboration within different departments in the same secondary school impacted upon the learning of the teachers. Where these departments were assessed as being more closely collaborative, greater informal opportunities were observed as part of the daily lives of the teachers involved.

The concept of expansive and restrictive learning environments was initially developed by Fuller and Unwin (2004, 2006) and Fuller et al. (2005), who observed considerable differences in the quality of learning for apprentices in different firms in the steel industry. These differences were considered to be a result of the variation in quality of the learning environments. I define an expansive learning environment to be one in which we experience a wide range of diverse opportunities to learn and we have a staff team that values and actively supports learning. A restrictive learning environment is one in which staff are potentially competing and are not collaborative and supportive of each other's professional learning. Factors such as performance-related pay and hierarchical structures in schools can serve to promote competition and inhibit collaboration amongst teachers.

When I arrived at my current school, the environment did not support collaboration amongst teachers. Experienced teachers did not have the time to support less-experienced teachers because they themselves felt under pressure and judged on the progress of their own 30 children. Low pupil outcomes across the school and an imminent Ofsted inspection meant that teachers did not feel they had the time to focus on anything other than their own classrooms – most team leaders and phase leaders were focused on telling colleagues what to do in a culture of hierarchy and compliance. A large number of inexperienced teachers certainly had the will and motivation to improve, but not the learning opportunities. As soon as I arrived I knew that I needed to tap into this and create a more-expansive learning environment.

Consider the extent to which the learning environment in your school: provides opportunities for collaborative working; is genuinely mutually supportive; supports opportunities to learn from practice in other schools; and offers opportunities to work in different groups. These activities may seem simple, but they are fundamental pillars in the construction and development of the thinking school. I have often thought to myself that it's a pretty simple and unremarkable finding from my eight years of research on teacher learning. I actively look for opportunities to get teachers to work in different groups on different projects – as always, with a focus on pupil learning. What opportunities do teachers at your school get to work with teachers in different groups?

As a class teacher myself, working with very challenging groups of children, I would always seek to give my pupils opportunities to work with a range of children across the class. This impacted positively on both the emotional and collaborative learning climate within the classroom. It is not simply a case of giving time and space to work together. Consider the extent to which this collaborative work enables discussions and evaluations of progress, with a critical reflection upon practice. Changes to teacher learning and practice can only take place when collaborative learning experiences provide opportunities for critical reflection.

Recently, three of our less-experienced teachers came together to lead a speechmaking competition across the local authority. They had never worked in the same phase of the school previously, with one teacher from Reception, one from Key Stage 1 and one from Key Stage 2. They had to project-manage the competition, including designing the advertising, training staff from participating schools, and coordinating the presentation event at a local secondary school. They worked collaboratively to make it a success and it has now been installed as an annual event. This learning activity for the trio involved high challenge, high trust and ongoing collaborative dialogue and reflection upon practice.

The learning community within your school is made up of individuals and it is the extent to which they are individually positive, supportive and collaborative that maintains the collective expansive learning environment. Leaders are pivotal in creating a group climate for learning even when individuals may be resistant. The learning environment can act as a mechanism to even out individual differences and foster collaborative learning. Ensure that team members have shared goals which are dependent on collaboration for their successful attainment. Leaders are critical in promoting and modelling collaborative learning, and the commitment of your headteacher and senior leaders will make the difference between environments that are supportive to professional learning and those that constrain it.

Schools make decisions on the allocation of resources to support teacher learning both within and beyond the school and the practical activities that are provided to support teacher learning. Financial management is important because highly successful schools and school systems invest in their teachers. Examples of these investment activities include opportunities for: observing others; mentoring and coaching; collaborative working; and taking risks and making mistakes. Leaders have the ability to influence both the learning activities that take place within your school and the positive and public support for teacher learning. The informal role of leaders within the school, their interpersonal skills and commitment to continual learning are significant factors. Leaders should model the learning mentality and the collaborative learning relationships they wish to foster and replicate amongst their staff. My role is crucial in modelling learning skills to staff. If I want my staff to be creative, reflective risk-takers, I have to model these skills in my leadership of learning.

Crucial to the development of a staff team is the development of individuals who want to be the best they can be and are open to collaboration, learning and development. So how do you enable every teacher to see themselves as a learner who wants to develop and grow in a way that the teacher you imagined in chapter 1 would?

Promoting positive individual dispositions to learning

The development of a thinking school is not easy and I don't want to give the impression that by simply initiating a set of strategies, every teacher automatically develops the personal and professional skills equivalent to the best teacher that you have worked with. You implement the structures that influence the learning culture in a school, and this will positively influence teachers' learning dispositions. Through engagement in key activities, they begin to see that their own learning is crucial in supporting children's learning. Every teacher needs to have this learning mentality if the school is to be collectively successful. Have faith in the model and over time you will see continual improvement. You are developing teachers and building learning capacity amongst the collective staff team within the thinking school, and it will take some colleagues longer than others.

I often tell my teachers that they are only as successful as the child that achieves the least. A parent is not interested in the progress of all the other children in the class if their own child is not progressing in their learning. As a school leader, judge yourself by the least effective teacher in the school. The children in that class will not benefit from excellent practice in other classrooms. We aim for consistency of practice across the school through collaborative teacher learning. As a school leader, I am only satisfied if I would be happy for any of my own children to be placed in any class in my school. If any class teacher in the school is not currently good enough for your own children, then why should they be good enough for anybody else's? By encouraging collaborative learning, we even out individual differences in the quality of teaching and raise the standard for all.

The term 'individual dispositions to learning' demonstrates that teachers have individual agency in the extent to which they engage in the learning opportunities on offer in the workplace. Although I encourage every teacher to undertake a Master's in Education, I cannot expect all teachers to instinctively want to engage in research. It is my job to demonstrate the value to staff of engagement in learning and development of practice. Consider the motivations of your staff. A key motivator should be to improve practice, to become a better teacher.

We began by giving every teacher the opportunity to undertake MA study, including part-funding their research. When setting our budget each year, we ensure that a significant sum is targeted at teacher learning. There are two aspects to encouraging master's-level study. Firstly, if one teacher is undertaking a master's, the benefit to the school goes beyond the teacher. That teacher's engagement will have a positive impact on other colleagues in the school, especially if there are wider opportunities for collaborative working. Secondly, as teachers hear their colleagues discussing their enjoyment in master's-level study and see the improvements they have made to their practice, they see the value of undertaking an MA themselves even if they had been reluctant at first.

Most of the teachers at our school who have completed their MA had no previous motivation to undertake one. It is usually easier to encourage new entrants to the profession to begin an MA, perhaps because they have been accustomed to study and completing assignments. Often, but certainly not always, more-experienced practitioners can be more reluctant to make changes to their practice. We've all met people that I like to call the 'seen it all before brigade'. These teachers may be reluctant to make changes or perceived improvements to their practice because it somehow implies that what they were doing before was wrong. Encouraging teachers to engage in research through an MA can serve to ease these anxieties.

Foster a culture that says that we are constantly striving to improve our practice year-on year. I know that the quality of teachers' marking is better now than it was when I first started as a teacher. I do not judge myself negatively because I know I was doing my best at the time. However, our knowledge about effective feedback has quite rightly improved during that period and I'm certain that in ten years' time, the quality of marking and feedback will have improved even further.

When we buy a new car, we expect it to be an improvement on the previous model that we owned. For example, better safety features or improved technology. There are too many fixed ideas in teaching and not enough teacher-led research-based practice. If you want teachers to make changes to their practice, don't just tell them what to do. To implement quality change, give teams of teachers time to work collaboratively to explore and trial changes to their practice. This will enable teachers to develop practices that they believe in. Teachers will then be motivated to engage in and drive their own and others' learning.

A number of writers (for examples, see Hodkinson and Hodkinson, 2004, 2005; Fuller et al., 2005; Evans et al., 2006) have referred to the influence of past experiences and individuals' dispositions to learning on directing teachers' engagement in the learning opportunities offered in the workplace. These experiences influence those thousands of decisions that teachers make every day. Hodkinson and Hodkinson (2004) have shown that an individual's disposition is partly constructed through their experiences in the workplace, as well as their own life experiences.

We are all likely to have worked with some colleagues who are super positive and optimistic regarding both the job that they do and the children they work with. And we've all probably worked with colleagues who are very much the opposite. Who would you rather work with?

Someone once described these two types of workers to me as 'radiators' and 'drains'.

Now take the example of workplace experiences. We are limited in the extent to which we can directly influence the life experiences of workers, but we can definitely influence their workplace experiences. Actively demonstrate to staff the type of teacher that you value in your school – one who is committed to continually growing and developing. As the team grows and develops with learning-focused leaders, the culture in the school strengthens as new entrants join. People want to stay in our school, so we retain our excellent staff. Like-minded people, with a strong learning mentality, want to join the school.

The learning community gets stronger and stronger, with an energy for continual learning and development. In a perpetually difficult climate for retention and recruitment, the thinking school will thrive. Each year, we have more teachers that want to join the school than we have vacancies. If you work closely with your local Initial Teacher Training providers, you should ideally have a range of student teachers working in your school over the course of a year. They will see how motivated practitioners at your school are and how valued teacher learning is. To date, in six years of headship, we have spent a grand total of £28 on recruitment and advertising. And that £28 was an advert for a new member of staff for our office team.

Every member of staff is unique and their attitudes to learning will differ. Ensure that leaders in your school view the staff that they are leading in the same way that you expect a class teacher to view their children. I view the 30 teachers that I lead in the school in the same way that I expect each teacher to view their children. I expect my teachers to know and understand each child, including their motivators. I want them to know each child as an individual, and their social, personal, emotional and academic learning needs. I want them to know exactly where those children are in their learning, and challenge them sufficiently and expertly to enable them to move on in an accelerated way. I expect my teachers to provide an environment that is calm and nurturing, with personalised learning opportunities for each child to develop as independent, lifelong learners. My responsibilities to the staff team are exactly the same. My greatest responsibility (beyond safeguarding of children) is to lead teacher learning, because of the direct influence on children's learning.

Values are important in schools because we are shaping and influencing the lives of children. It's different from working in a factory or building cars and our values influence our attitudes to children's learning. Your workplace learning experiences contribute to the development of your values and attitudes, and teacher learning activities need to include an emphasis on the development of positive values and attitudes both to your own learning and the learning of your children.

Encourage your teachers to take creative risks with their learning and practice. Teacher learning and making changes to practice can be an uncomfortable process for teachers. I have even found teachers who feel that networking is an unnecessary imposition, reflecting their negative attitudes towards the value of collaboration. These opportunities for networking can often degenerate into 'moan-fests' or an excuses culture for children's underachievement. Leaders need to show that they are open to change and to take risks with their own practice. One teacher once said to me that the thing that impressed her most was the extent to which I was able to acknowledge my own mistakes in my practice. This liberated her to be more creative and to take more risks with her practice. This approach meant that her children went on to make far greater progress over the course of a single year than her previous experiences when 'playing safe'. No one can teach perfect lessons all day every day – consistently good practice over time makes the greatest difference to children.

Be open to change and developing practice. I articulate it to staff as an 80/20 process. 80% of our excellent practice should remain the same each year – for example, our commitment to maintaining excellent learning relationships with our children and our commitment to collaborative working with each other. But we should also be open to innovating with 20% of your practice in our quest for improvement. Teacher commitment to professional learning and reflective practice cannot be taken for granted. For example, experienced teachers may say that they don't need to learn more about topics such as assessment for learning or guided reading, for example, because they may see themselves as experts. They should be encouraged to innovate and engage in whole-school professional learning topics. The development of positive teacher learning activities will influence teacher engagement, and this is particularly significant for NQTs. Positive early workplace learning experiences will enable positive attitudes and this will continue to develop through their work histories.

Individual teachers will influence the quality of the learning environment in your school, and the learning environment will in turn influence individual teachers' attitudes to learning. As the learning community grows and replicates itself, eventually all teachers will have excellent attitudes to learning. Every year, members of staff have left our school and new staff have joined. The staff that remain develop even greater attitudes to their learning, and the staff that join are equally committed and positive. Teachers' attitudes are influenced by each other and they promote the culture for learning across the school.

The value of distributed leadership

I have explained that every member of staff within the thinking school should see themselves as a leader. This is because when you lead, you have to think wider and bring your brain to work. You have to be aware of the impact of your actions upon others, as well as a wider responsibility to the institution. Once we develop a core sense of shared values and understand our collective responsibilities, we all become capable of making leadership decisions in relation to the institution. Leadership is also related to learning and growth. The more we have opportunities to lead, the more we learn about ourselves, our colleagues and our school, and it supports our growth as leaders of learning. I hear school leaders describe how they have distributed leadership in their schools. However, often this just involves delegating jobs and titles – for example, subject leaders. I question the extent to which these middle leader roles are more likely to involve managing rather than leading – tidying stock cupboards or purchasing resources rather than leading children's learning in that subject across the school. We have to be confident that if we are all doing our jobs effectively, an NQT will be able to make leadership decisions that reflect the ethos of the school.

Authentic distributed leadership requires you to delegate the decision-making responsibilities to staff – opportunities to innovate, develop and lead practice in their area of leadership. Many schools are characterised by very hierarchical leadership structures, with large senior leadership teams (SLTs). They make decisions regarding the curriculum and teaching and learning policies, for example, and teachers are then expected to carry out these policies in the classroom. Members of the SLT will then monitor the teachers to evaluate the extent to which these policies have been carried out. This type of micromanagement does not encourage a positive climate for teacher learning and growth.

Having a smaller 'so-called' senior leadership team enables us to more effectively distribute teaching and learning responsibilities across a wider range of staff. When I arrived at the school I realised that many of the leadership responsibilities undertaken by the two deputies I inherited could easily be undertaken by skilled members of the office team. Take every opportunity possible to examine the roles and responsibilities of your staff team to ensure that all staff are being challenged to work to their full potential.

Enable your staff to use their developing knowledge and experience to both make decisions as leaders and empower others. Empowerment of those very workers that are at the front line of the institution (teachers) is the key to continual improvement. Conceptions of workplace learning in Japanese industries are very different from traditional conceptions of workplace learning in Western management models. Nonaka and Takeuchi (1995) have described how the centrepiece of the Japanese approach to worker learning and the development of practice was to tap into the tacit knowledge of workers on the front line.

Key to this is each individual teacher's alignment with and commitment to the central goals and values of the organisation, and their willingness to collaborate with colleagues to develop practice. In Japanese companies, the ultimate aim is to improve the quality of the product and productivity. Our goal in schools is to improve the quality of pupil learning. The extent to which workers in Japanese companies have a sense of collective identity is critical, as it is in the thinking school. We must work together to improve. Knowledge-creation for workers is crucial – make your teachers responsible for reflecting, adapting and improving practice. Also critical in Japanese companies is the opportunity for workers to set their own goals, and the role of senior managers is to enable teams to set goals and meet them.

The appraisal system in most schools is typically hierarchical. We have got to the point where each member of staff writes their own appraisal targets and each year group team sets their own collective pupil progress targets. This requires each individual to consider their own learning and development needs as well as those of the children that they are working with. Encourage your staff to set challenging targets and they will be more motivated to work individually and collectively to achieve them. We believe that it is better to set a more challenging target and just miss it than it is to set and meet a more conservative target. In most examples, teachers revise their pupil progress targets upwards during the course of the year. We also include mid-year appraisals to discuss successes and challenges. The role of the line manager is therefore to support and enable their colleague to succeed within a shared culture of high expectations for teachers' and children's learning. Make your year group leaders the appraisers for their team members. Once teams have established their challenging targets, leave them to creatively reflect and experiment with their practice to meet those targets.

Empowerment is what learning-focused leaders promote, so encourage your leaders to share authority with members of their team. We take equal responsibility for every success and every failure. This empowerment is designed to create a positive collective energy that is simply not possible in hierarchical structures where senior teams have all the responsibility. Whilst leadership is indeed distributed through delegated responsibilities in schools, it is not always distributed in a way that empowers staff. Schools have a great deal to learn from workplaces in which all workers are encouraged to be creative and to take leadership responsibilities. An authentically distributed leadership model within schools can empower all staff within the school to see themselves as leaders and develop leadership skills. These leaders are then empowered to make decisions that are aligned to the central vision of the school and staff members are encouraged to be continually reflective and creative in their thinking and practice. Too often in hierarchical structures, teachers can be left feeling isolated in the classroom because they are unclear of what is expected of them.

Give your teachers a voice in making decisions about the core activity of learning and teaching. The first rule of distributed leadership is that everyone has a voice. A major difficulty that many teachers face is that they don't always feel able to speak up. I have heard countless frustrations expressed by teachers regarding lesson observations by senior leaders. The lesson observation is seen as judgemental and performance-related, rather than a developmental learning opportunity to better understand pupil learning and improve practice. This is even more difficult when the relationship between the observer and the teacher is one-way in terms of arriving at judgements and setting targets. Many teachers would like to see the observer demonstrating and modelling teaching skills and strategies rather than simply giving instructions on what to do.

I have highlighted below four key areas of responsibility that underpin the distributed leadership structure: equal responsibility; authentic responsibility; collaborative responsibility; and personalised responsibility.

Equal responsibility

As headteacher of a primary school, I don't see myself as more important than any other member of staff. It is not my job to tell people what to do. It is a leader's job to inspire and motivate them to believe that all members of the staff team within the institution have the same goals, and that these goals are concerned with the social, personal and academic learning of all children. Staff are not doing something because their headteacher has told them to do it, but because everybody believes that it is the right thing to do in line with the collective vision of the school. Make the vision and values for your school so vivid and strong that every person can effectively make leadership decisions.

Reflect on your collective practice and ensure that your conversations focus on pupil learning and how you impact upon this. Learn from both the positive and negative experiences in your school, within a blame-free culture. If everyone has a voice and is able to share their experiences and opinions, you are making full use of all the collective experience of the staff. Equal responsibility is about every member of staff being both valued and accountable.

In my second year of headship, one of my teachers sent me an electronic link regarding the value of philosophy teaching to children's mental wellbeing. I responded to her by saying that I thought the research article was interesting and that she should investigate further. She took the opportunity to undertake further research and evaluate best practice in philosophy teaching. She then went on to set up a team and wrote an action plan for the implementation of philosophy across the school.

Her learning-focused leadership meant that it was introduced and embedded across the school. By the second year, she was providing model lessons for teachers across the LA and presenting at national conferences. She has recently become the first specialist leader of education (SLE) for philosophy in the LA. I could have provided several similar examples of teacher leadership. My role is clear in that I want to provide an environment in which teachers are encouraged to follow their passions. Their job is to provide creative energy and it is my job to give them the time, space and resources to succeed. In the above example, this included covering her class to enable her to provide model lessons to other teachers. Equal responsibility also means that skilled teaching assistants can effectively cover classes for short periods to enable these types of professional learning activities.

Authentic responsibility

If you truly want your staff to lead, give them the opportunity to do all the things that great leaders do. Great leaders take risks, they innovate, and they are always seeking to improve and make changes to their practice. When teachers are given leadership responsibilities, are they really encouraged to do these things? Or is it more a case of ensuring that all the boxes have been ticked in preparation for Ofsted? If you are going to give leadership responsibilities but constantly monitor their work, you stifle learning. Leaders need to feel able to make decisions in leading their year groups or subjects, and this has to happen in a culture of high trust as well as high accountability. This will build social capital and confidence amongst staff.

When I hold leaders accountable for their work, I do so in terms of their impact upon children's learning outcomes. You can spend all day monitoring teachers' planning, observing lessons, undertaking book scrutinies, evaluating quality of marking – the list is endless. However, all of those activities mentioned above should only have one goal: to enable your children to make excellent progress in their learning. Set high standards for your teachers. Because of the significant investment in quality teacher learning experiences, I expect teachers in our school to be more reflective, more knowledgeable, more skilled, and therefore ultimately more effective than the average teacher in England. If every teacher at the school is performing above average (and above average for attendance and wellbeing), and we believe that the greatest impact on the quality of children's learning is teaching, then the children that attend our school for seven years will make excellent progress.

Every teacher is aware that this is the goal, and planning, marking and feedback are just some of the tools that make this positive difference to children's learning. Authentic responsibility is about teachers suggesting ideas, looking at alternative theories, taking risks and ultimately, taking responsibility for the learning of the children that they are accountable for. As a leader, I try to break high-impact learning activities into simple ideas. Put simply, I have a responsibility to the staff that I lead and they have a responsibility to me, centred on children's learning. We both want every child to make excellent progress as a learner.

If I relate this idea to my relationship with a team leader, for example, we both have a responsibility to ensure that all 90 children in the year group make excellent progress. Once we have collectively set our challenging targets, I define our individual responsibilities in a simple way. I have a responsibility to support the team leader with tools and resources to enable them to achieve this aim, and they have a responsibility to ensure that they are direct and timely in saying whether there are any barriers to achieving that progress. This ensures that we collectively maintain our focus on children's learning throughout the year. This approach ensures that our children's progress across all subjects is consistently in the top 10% of schools nationally.

Collaborative responsibility

No single leader in a school, including the headteacher, should ever feel that they have sole responsibility. All decisions should be made collaboratively and based upon authentic professional dialogue. Decisions made by leaders are based on the effective co-construction of knowledge about where the school is in terms of strengths and areas for development – and what changes need to be implemented to move the school on. Activities such as informal and formal professional conversations, a coaching culture and peer learning will ensure that all staff seize on opportunities to take risks, make mistakes – and crucially, learn! This enables the development of a collaborative learning culture that welcomes challenge and a positive 'can do' attitude within the school.

I consult with different members of staff on every decision that I take. This enables me to explore a range of perspectives before I make a decision. However, this decision does not need to be discussed with everyone at a designated leadership meeting. I will select key people to discuss certain ideas with. I encourage all staff to work in this way so that everyone feels that they can contribute to leadership decisions. When I first arrived at the school, senior leaders felt undermined if I consulted a teacher about something before I had spoken to them. This seemed very inflexible to me and I felt that it hampered effective and timely school improvement. These attitudes were more about the egos of leaders rather than the needs of teachers and children. Ensure that you are always working in the best interests and needs of the children at your school.

Collaborative responsibility ensures that all activities that teams engage in are focused on children's learning. This includes working together as a team at the beginning of the year to write an action plan and set clear and challenging goals for children's learning. All subsequent collaborative conversations and activities during the year are then focused on the extent to which the objectives on the action plan have been achieved. Teachers within a year group have collective responsibility for all 90 children, not just for their own 30 children – and this is very important. This collective responsibility also promotes staff wellbeing as individuals do not feel isolated and are made to feel part of a team. Collaborative learning activities within the team include: planning together; visiting each other's classrooms; engaging in collaborative action research; evaluating pupil learning together through book scrutinies; evaluating data. We accept our mistakes together as a team and celebrate our successes as a team.

Personalised responsibility

A headteacher should view their staff in the same way that a class teacher views their children. Just as all children are different and their individual learning needs need to be taken into consideration, it is the same for staff. Ensure you are inclusive and that staff are valued for their individual skills and achievements, and are supported to continue to learn. Challenge your staff to be the best that they can possibly be. Many of the responsibilities held by senior leaders within schools – for example, timetabling, organisation of cover, data collection, premises etc. – should be the responsibility of a highly skilled office team. This enables all leaders within the distributed model to focus on the core business of learning and teaching. Within this model, all teaching staff – including the headteacher – would have to teach. One of the first things I did as a headteacher was to ensure, as far as possible, that all admin tasks were delegated to office staff. This liberated all teaching staff to focus on teaching and learning.

It's important that leaders are able to understand the experiences of all the staff that they lead. How can you understand what it is like to be a cleaner, a midday assistant, or site supervisor in your school? Until I had worked in the kitchen, serving food at lunchtime, I did not realise how physically challenging it was. Understand the professional learning experiences of the staff that you lead, and lead their learning and development in such a way that they feel valued. Recognise when it may be appropriate to change individual leaders' responsibilities at the school. As staff in your school experience a range of leadership responsibilities, the collective knowledge and experience amongst the staff will grow.

If every member of staff is a leader, that means they could be leading a different subject or a different year group each year. In the past three years, I have worked with some highly skilled team leaders. I have deliberately made someone else in the year group team leader to enable others to develop their leadership skills. Meanwhile, this has enabled established team leaders to develop a wider range of leadership skills, and prevents people becoming pigeonholed as the maths coordinator or PE lead. In our school, any member of the staff team can lead the Monday morning whole-school briefing, and anyone can attend the half-termly headteachers' local authority briefing. It may be difficult to envisage, but in the thinking school, it can happen.

Summary

In this third chapter, I have discussed the importance of establishing a learning environment in your school that enables you to maximise the available formal and informal professional learning opportunities. I have detailed the significance of school leaders in directly determining the expansiveness of the learning environment, and introduced the concept of learning-focused leadership. In the thinking school, all members of staff should be seen as leaders. Learning-focused leaders take their own learning seriously, actively seeking out opportunities to reflect upon and improve their practice. They also have an unfailing focus on children's learning, using it as a barometer to measure their own effectiveness. Leadership is led by our values, which in turn inform our actions. The stronger the sense of shared purpose and values, the stronger the collective effectiveness of staff.

Learning-focused leaders in the thinking school are collaborative and inclusive. Leaders implement teacher learning activities that enable the development of staff, and their interpersonal skills are significant in setting the emotional climate in the school. These teacher learning activities and the emotional climate at the school will both influence teachers' individual dispositions to learning. My research highlighted the significance of individual teachers' life and work experiences in shaping their dispositions to learning. These dispositions can be more or less positive and influence the extent to which individual teachers elect to engage in the learning opportunities on offer. But these learning dispositions are not fixed and an expansive learning environment influences teachers' dispositions to learning. An authentic distributed leadership model is essential in enabling staff to learn and develop as leaders.

Relevant reading

Billett, S. (2006) 'Constituting the workplace curriculum', *Journal of Curriculum Studies* 38 (1) pp. 31–48.

Evans, K., Hodkinson, P., Rainbird, H and Unwin, L. (2006) *Improving workplace learning*. Abingdon: Routledge.

Fuller, A. and Unwin, L. (2004) 'Expansive learning environments: integrating personal and organizational development' in Rainbird, H., Fuller, A. and Munro, A. (eds) *Workplaces learning in context*. London: Routledge, pp. 126–144.

Fuller, A., Hodkinson, H., Hodkinson, P. and Unwin, L. (2005) 'Learning as peripheral participation in communities of practice: a reassessment of key concepts in workplace learning', *British Educational Research Journal* 31 (1) pp. 49–68.

Fuller, A. and Unwin, L. (2006) 'Expansive and restrictive learning environments' in Evans, L., Hodkinson, P., Rainbird, H. and Unwin, L. (eds) *Improving workplace learning*. London: Routledge, pp. 27–48.

Hodkinson, P. and Hodkinson, H. (2004) 'The significance of individuals' dispositions in workplace learning: a case study of two teachers', *Journal of Education and Work* 17 (2) pp. 167–182.

Hodkinson, H. and Hodkinson, P. (2005) 'Improving schoolteachers' workplace learning', *Research Papers in Education* 20 (2) pp. 109–131.

Lave, J. and Wenger, E. (1991) *Situated learning*. Cambridge: Cambridge University Press.

Nonaka, I. and Takeuchi, H. (1995) *The knowledge-creating company: how Japanese companies create the dynamics of innovation*. New York, NY: Oxford University Press.

Robinson, V. (2011) *Student-centered leadership*. San Francisco, CA: Jossey-Bass.

Reflective questions

1. Are there activities in school that distract you from focusing on children's learning?

2. To what extent do you think the staff in your school share core beliefs and values?

3. How expansive do you think the learning environment is for teachers in your school?

4. What further professional learning opportunities would you like teachers at your school to engage in?

5. How would you describe your own dispositions to learning?

6. What is your personal perspective on the value of an authentic distributed leadership model in your school?

Chapter 4

Activities in the thinking school

We have established why we need to create thinking schools and how school leaders can develop an expansive learning environment that maximises the formal and informal professional learning opportunities available to teachers. In this chapter I detail two key professional learning activities that teachers require so that they can develop their practice, namely engagement in action research and peer learning/lesson study. Peer learning and lesson study go together because lesson study is an enhanced form of peer learning and teachers need experience of peer learning before they can successfully engage in lesson study. These professional learning activities enhance teachers' dispositions to learning and, consequently, enrich the learning environment. They will have a positive impact on engagement in informal learning activities, such as collaborative professional dialogue between teachers that emphasises children's learning.

Two key areas of pedagogy are assessment for learning and dialogic talk for learning. Remember that we want our teachers to be thinkers so they can in turn influence their children's thinking. Ultimately, we want children, too, to be creative thinkers and develop a passion for independent learning. Assessment for learning and dialogic teaching are continually explored and developed by teachers engaged in action research. Teachers' own study empowers them to be reflective, thoughtful practitioners and to develop their craft knowledge. A key premise within the thinking school is that all learning happens through talk, so we encourage talk for staff and children alike.

Action research

I focus in particular on action research because my doctoral thesis investigated teacher engagement in action research. However, all forms of practitioner engagement in research are of value. All teachers should engage in research to develop their knowledge, understanding and skills and to improve their practice, and research should be fundamental in the teacher's role. My own experiences and engagement in research significantly improved my practice. If all teachers conducted action research, the learning community at your school would be engaged in continual improvement. My experiences as a school leader and my encouragement of teacher research has only confirmed this.

I promote action research because I want teachers to engage in and develop evidence-informed practice. I discussed earlier how teachers make thousands of decisions every day – which question to ask, which child to choose, what response to give. I want teachers to understand the factors that influence their decision-making. Many of these decisions are influenced by our prior work and life experiences, and are made unconsciously. Action research is about reflecting on our practice, trialling new ideas and evaluating their success. It enables each teacher to understand what is working well and what can be done to improve their practice.

In their continuing professional learning, teachers are encouraged to continually develop and adapt their professional practice. Evaluate the extent to which your school affords teachers (individually or in groups) opportunities to learn and reflect. Hoban (2002) has argued that there is a paradox in the teaching profession because many teachers are reluctant to change their practice, even though their teaching must respond to a rapidly changing society. A researcher once told me that one project he worked on found that many teachers stopped improving their practice beyond their third year of teaching.

There is some debate surrounding children's educational experiences regarding the extent to which we should be teaching knowledge or teaching skills. Children need knowledge but they also need to develop metacognitive learning and thinking skills. They need to be able to learn and adapt to the many changes they will face in their lives, and our expectations for teachers should be the same. Ensure that your professional learning activities are enabling teachers to develop their skills as well as their knowledge.

One teacher working in Year 6 at our school managed to complete her master's by the end of her second year in teaching. This meant that she was continually engaged in action research in her classroom during this period. She was always reflecting upon her own practice and her impact upon children's learning. Her NQT year required her to adapt to a new curriculum and assessment procedures for the children. She was able to face these challenges in a confident and informed way. During those two years, pupil progress figures for the children she was teaching were in line with the top 10% of schools nationally. When she was initially placed in Year 6 for her NQT year, her colleagues on her teacher training course asked if her headteacher was mad! I was confident that her dispositions and attitudes to learning would enable her to be successful. I was also confident that the structures we had in place, allied to the learning culture in the thinking school, would ensure that she would grow and develop. Through action research, she has developed the skills to be a reflective practitioner and this will support her to develop throughout her teaching career.

Kraft and Papay's (2014) analysis showed that teachers working in supportive professional environments improved their effectiveness more over time than those working in less-supportive environments. A 2007 study jointly commissioned by the General Teaching Council for England (GTCE) and the Association of Teachers and Lecturers (ATL) aimed to summarise different research and evaluation reports that had been commissioned by government agencies to evaluate teachers' professional learning. The report presented some significant assertions about the design of effective professional learning activities. Effective teacher learning involved:

- sustained interactions and interventions (as opposed to individual training sessions).
- affording teachers choice and influence over their professional development.
- activities designed to take account of the individual needs and priorities of teachers at different stages of their professional lives and careers.
- collaborative work within a professional learning community.

(General Teaching Council for England, 2007, p. 5)

A recent review of teachers' professional learning (Cordingley et al., 2015) shows that teacher learning is still not sufficiently sustained over time. Nor is it evidence-based. And teachers are not given enough choice in their learning. CPL leaders should take these findings into account when developing collaborative action research in their school so that it meets the professional learning needs of teachers and supports whole-school improvement.

In my first term as headteacher, I had to rapidly make improvements to the consistency and quality of teaching and the children's learning experiences. The term was therefore spent with all year groups engaging in sustained collaborative research projects. The overarching theme for development across the school was assessment for learning, and each year group analysed their cohorts of children to identify an aspect of practice related to assessment for learning that they wished to explore and develop.

In my work over the years, action research is the methodology I use for school-based teacher inquiry because its design equips teachers with practical methods for developing knowledge from their experiences in the classroom. Action research for teachers has developed from the work of Stenhouse (1975), whose model of 'teacher as researcher' was very much about teachers valuing the importance of lifelong learning. An evaluation of educational researchers' perspectives on action research reveals that there are conflicting views as to what constitutes action research. However, the literature on action research clearly emphasises the researcher actively participating in the study and investigating changes to their practice.

If we relate this to a teacher, their role as a researcher is to intentionally change and improve their class teaching. Unlike many research methodologies, therefore, a measurement of the outcomes of the research is valued less in terms of the theories generated and much more in terms of the changes made to practice. I would define the process of action research for teachers as research that they lead, that aims to attain personal and pupil learning, and that enables them to find answers to complex questions within the contexts of their classrooms and schools. For a teacher to engage in action research, they identify a problem that they would like to investigate. They undertake relevant reading and consider an action they can undertake to improve their practice. They implement the action and evaluate the impact on children's learning. They then adjust their future practice to reflect their findings.

A number of researchers (e.g. McNiff and Whitehead, 2005; Elliot, 2007) have adapted action research to define a methodology specifically designed for individual teachers to undertake research within their own educational settings. They have investigated the use of cyclical models for learning through action research, which involve the researcher in planning, reflecting, observing, revising and then repeating the cycle. This model of action research is promoting a process of action and reflection designed to improve practice. Teachers gain from the accessibility of action research: they needn't necessarily have a background in research to engage in action research. Action research, as detailed here, is defined as professional learning of teachers, enabling them to learn about the school environment in the school environment in order to develop and improve practice.

Teacher engagement in action research

As part of my research, I evaluated a range of research studies in an attempt to identify the potential benefits for teacher engagement in action research, as well as the potential challenges. My research informed the conceptual development of the dynamic learning community in the school. I found that participating in research transformed the professional learning experience for teachers who were accustomed to having only piecemeal professional learning activities, as is so often the case. The studies of teachers engaging in research identified factors that clearly promoted quality teacher learning in schools: collaborative working; working in a variety of groups; mutual support between colleagues; a school culture where teacher learning became an embedded feature of classroom practice.

The studies that specifically evaluate the relationship between school-based action research and professional learning agree on its potential: learning is readily accessible to teachers; their practice improves; the impact on children, parents and colleagues is positive; teachers' reflection and learning can be sustained; teacher autonomy and professionalism grows; individual, institutional and cultural change is supported; and teachers' wellbeing and personal development are supported. However, the research evidence also demonstrates the likely impediments, such as: conflicting government initiatives; inadequate leadership and institutional support in schools; lack of external expertise; the complexity of research processes; resistance by some teachers; teachers' stressful workloads and shortage of time.

It is clear that collaboratively engaging in research with colleagues and taking time to reflect upon their practice greatly benefits teachers. It enables teachers to have a greater sense of self-efficacy and confidence. I have always been particularly keen on implementing action research in the schools that I have worked in because I want to shift teachers away from external factors to factors they are in control of in the classroom – away from socio-economic and cultural factors that affect children's learning and towards the expansive and pedagogically informed learning experiences they can offer in the classroom.

Action research enables us to think proactively about our own role in enabling children's learning. When I arrived at my current school, the school was going through a period of low attainment and achievement across all Key Stages. When I was interviewed for the post, there were only four schools (out of 47) across the LA below them in the league tables. I certainly did not think this was reflective of where they should be, and I was given a range of excuses for this clear underachievement. Action research enables us to move away from a blame culture to one in which we consider, trial and evaluate every possible strategy to secure improvement. We do not let excuses or underachievement define us.

When I first asked the teachers to engage in collaborative action research, each year group had to identify a particular concern that they had about their children. Several teachers discussed how they viewed the children as passive learners, voicing their concern that these children didn't engage in whole-class teaching. Some teachers even discussed their passivity in terms of cultural or gender norms and expectations. I was shocked that one teacher in particular did not appreciate her own role in making the children passive. When visiting her class, I could see that many children were indeed not contributing to whole-class discussions. However, this was not because they were somehow naturally passive. They were feeling a combination of fear and boredom. This was a Year 1 class and I'm certain the children would not have been as passive when they arrived in Nursery or Reception.

We must look at ourselves and accept our own influence in children's achievement and underachievement. I have had the privilege of visiting classrooms across the world and I have seen many children behaving in a passive way. However, this is more often because of the quality of teaching and its inability to engage and motivate the children. One person once told me that children learn more between the ages of 0 and 3 than at any other time in their lives. They learn to walk and are able to communicate in multiple languages. Consider how many times a child falls over whilst learning to walk. They may learn to walk at different rates but all children get there eventually. Children are creative, imaginative and resilient and are natural-born learners. For many children, the first time that they begin to doubt themselves as learners is when they come to school and receive feedback from adults. In all your interactions with children, consider how you are developing their self-esteem as learners.

In every class that I have taught, I can broadly break the class up into four groups. Let's consider them as 30%, 30%, 30% and 10%.

- The first group of 30% comprises children that are suited to learning in a school environment. They would still learn relatively successfully if an inexperienced student teacher were taking the class. They would be able to access sufficient resources to learn independently.

- The second group are children who could be just as successful as the first group. They may not have as much support or access to resources at home, or they may have some additional personal or emotional needs. A skilled teacher will effectively motivate and engage these children to learn and succeed.

- The fourth group of children in any school are those children with specific identified special learning needs (SEN). They will need the curriculum adapted to meet their particular needs, and may require specialist additional adult interventions.

- Really successful schools are defined by the progress they make with the third group of learners. Only the most skilled teachers will enable these children to make equal levels of attainment and progress in learning as the first two groups.

These children in group three are often wrongly characterised as SEN. When I arrived at my school, over 20% of the children were classified as SEN – now it's less than 10%. Give all children opportunities to talk about their learning, thinking and misconceptions. This third group of children can achieve very well if they have teachers who understand their personal, social and academic learning needs. I expect every child that does not have a specified special need to achieve the expected national standards.

All members of staff need to share these aspirations and expectations. In 2011, only 60% of children at our school achieved the expected standards in English and maths. The expectation in standards for 11-year-olds has risen considerably in the years since. In 2017, 86% of our children achieved the expected standard across English and maths (in comparison to 61% nationally), placing us second in the LA. That figure rose to 87% in 2018. For that third group of children in 2017 and 2018, we were recognised by the Mayor of London as a 'School for Success' – one of only 46 primary and secondary schools across London to achieve that. This was awarded in recognition of the exceptional progress made by our low prior attainers. This success for children cannot happen in a single year (particularly not in their final year in school – in our case, Year 6) but is a reflection of consistently excellent practice over an extended period and high expectations for all.

Experience has taught me that engagement in collaborative action research has to be organised at whole-school level and involve all the staff. They need to be given a clear structure in which to organise their research. Action research is particularly valuable because it is not difficult for teachers to undertake. In my first year as headteacher, all the teachers engaged in two action research projects; one focusing on assessment for learning and the other on talk for learning. I chose these because I wanted to improve the quality of teaching and learning. With my research background, I could provide both a pro forma to frame their research and access to the relevant literature to inform their thinking, and I could lead professional learning meetings.

In the six years since we began, teachers have worked in partnership with our local university on a range of research projects focusing on different topics. Academic professionals can support you in organising action research projects across the school and in providing personalised challenge for individuals and groups of teachers. Examples have included modules on pedagogy, leadership, feedback, creativity, inclusion, and reading. For each module, teams of teachers had the opportunity to engage with relevant literature and design an action research study to develop their practice. Each team's findings were then shared with the whole staff and we used our collective findings to inform whole-school policy and practice. This has meant that our teachers' developing knowledge and understanding has informed our revised expectations and policies.

In reading for example, we have a specific model for guided reading that is consistently implemented in every classroom. In 2018, 93% of our children achieved the expected standard in reading, in comparison to 75% nationally. This is particularly significant when considering the fact that we are in the top 20% of schools nationally for mobility (high numbers of children leave and join our school each year, and many that join do not speak any English) and over 80% of our children speak English as an additional language. As the learning community matures, our teachers are able to draw upon a wider range of research methodologies.

At the time of writing, ten of our teachers have completed their MA, a further fifteen are on the journey, and two have begun their professional doctorates.

Engagement in research encourages collaborative learning, and through collaborative work with colleagues and academic partners, teachers are able to reflect upon their practice and become more knowledgeable about teaching and learning. Sharing experiences and reflections and gathering and evaluating data together all develop a wider learning community. Collaboration enables teachers to engage in professional dialogue and, even more importantly, empowers them to become more open about their practice. I remember vividly how well teachers collaborated on the pedagogy module and the impact across the school. Teachers creatively rearranged their classrooms to enable children's learning experiences to reflect the theories they had been researching. Teachers across the school were excitedly sharing their reflections and taking opportunities to visit each other's classrooms. They wanted to find out how colleagues were organising their classes to most effectively enable independent, paired and group learning. One outcome was the implementation of mixed-attaining groups of three children working on writing projects in Years 5 and 6.

Many of the studies I read described how action research developed teachers' autonomy and professionalism, crucial for teachers in successful schools. Teachers potentially become more knowledgeable and autonomous in their judgements. In our school, it makes my job easier to lead a team of master's graduates and teachers who are thoughtful and reflective about their practice. I found that the teachers' views changed about various aspects of teaching and learning and the expectations and role of the teacher.

Motivating teachers to research

We can't just expect teachers to engage in research. The research shows that teachers need to be motivated to engage. We know that collaboration and peer dialogue and observation are motivating activities for teachers. Other important influences include the following:

- Research that is relevant to teachers' day-to-day practice.
- Establishment of a culture of enquiry that respects the voice of teachers.
- Allowing opportunities and time to engage in theory and investigate practice.
- Focusing on initiatives that are known to be effective.
- Encouragement for teachers to identify their own focus.

Many studies into research motivation identified a major challenge for teachers: time and workload. Teachers felt that they needed time in their working lives to reflect upon their practice and to have professional discussions about it. Taking on and then sustaining research alongside their daily working routines was a daunting prospect. Therefore their engagement in research has to be so greatly valued that they are given time to do some research during the school day. The rewards will be increased teacher efficacy and improved practices. For every teacher in the school to be engaged in research requires institutional change, and this in turn requires recognition that quality change takes time. Evidence from Cordingley et al. (2015) suggests that if a school seeks to transform conceptions of teacher learning and make changes to accepted practices (as we did), such changes will take time. Learning communities need time to develop and become part of embedded practice, and there has to be a long-term commitment in the school.

School leaders are critical. It is they who develop the engagement, motivation and nurturing of teachers in action research and it is they who promote it. We saw in chapter 3 that leadership can make the difference between environments that constrain professional learning and those that are supportive. The leaders hold the pivotal role in providing a supportive environment in which teachers can successfully undertake and complete their research. Leaders also support the personal development of teachers through motivating and encouraging them. If staff believe that action research goes against the traditional models for teacher professional learning in schools, leaders have to be brave about pursuing it. At both my current and previous school, I went against the advice of LA advisers and consultants to ensure that all teachers engaged in research. I believed in the potential of action research in promoting teachers' long-term growth and deeper development – which I prefer to short-term fixes and shallow learning opportunities even though they demand more time.

I recall a conversation at a local network meeting for school leaders where I shared my enthusiasm for teacher research and our plans to part-fund each MA. One headteacher dismissed the idea and stated that he would never encourage his teachers to undertake an MA and would certainly not fund it. He questioned the value of supporting a teacher to complete an MA if they then went on to teach in another school. As leaders, we have a duty to develop teachers for the profession, not just for our own schools. Furthermore, I clearly see the value of supporting teachers to research, both in terms of school finances and children's outcomes. Not only are we a high-performing school, we are very effective in both retaining and recruiting our staff. Investing in our teachers' professional learning is a significant factor in this.

We organise collaborative action research studies twice in each academic year, one in the autumn term and the second in the summer term. The topic of study is informed by our own school self-evaluation and a module is designed in partnership with staff at the local university. However, we ensure that the topic of study allows enough flexibility for individual teachers and teams to make decisions about what they specifically wish to investigate.

We have four or five twilight sessions for each project led by the researchers and which all the teachers attend. During these sessions, teachers engage in reading, design an action research study, investigate their own practice using a range of research methods, and evaluate the impact on their own and their children's learning. Teachers who wish to submit a piece of writing for accreditation attend additional study support sessions. All sessions are held at the school, and the final session involves teachers sharing their learning with their colleagues to inform practice across the school. This whole-school engagement has had a transformational effect on teachers' and children's learning and development.

Peer lesson observations

Teachers in the thinking school should have as many opportunities as possible to engage in collaborative professional dialogue. The teachers continually reflect upon and improve their practice through collaborative lesson observations. It is a powerful way of enabling a greater consistency of practice and shared knowledge and understanding across the school. My own research found that teachers perceived peer lesson observation as a positive professional learning experience and they valued and enjoyed it. Teachers need to see themselves as peers and therefore equal participants, and the observation has to be undertaken properly within a clear structure where all participants feel safe. The legacy of lesson observations being a negative learning experience in England's schools must be challenged. A lesson observation undertaken in a hierarchical and judgemental way is the antithesis of collaborative practice.

Traditionally, lesson observation has been perceived as an opportunity for senior leaders to grade individual lessons, usually for accountability purposes in preparation for LA advisory visits or Ofsted inspections (although interestingly Ofsted have now stopped grading lessons). I have never graded a lesson as a senior leader in any school. Grading lessons can actually inhibit the professional learning experience for teachers. For example, if I knew that I was going to be observed as a class teacher, I would play safe and choose a lesson or subject that I was very familiar with and particularly confident in teaching. I would thus be maintaining my strengths and hiding my weaknesses. There was no incentive for me to ask to be observed teaching an area in which I was less confident (and therefore had greater capacity to grow and develop) because I would be worried about the judgement. If this feeling is replicated across the staff, then clearly lesson observations do not present an expansive learning opportunity. They don't encourage teachers to be creative, take risks, or learn and develop as peer learning is designed to do.

Peer learning in practice

In peer learning, one teacher observes another and feeds back, in a reflective way, on what they saw. The observing peer will focus on an area of practice that the teacher has identified as an area for improvement or further investigation. Introduce peer learning by allowing teachers to choose the peer they would like to work with in the first instance. We started by working within year groups, where the teams of teachers already planned collaboratively and could understand the learning outcomes across the year group. As the learning community matures and develops, all teachers become capable of working as peers. This is when you can progress on to lesson study. Our teachers engaged in three years of peer learning activities before we moved successfully onto lesson studies.

We found that peer learning was a particularly useful professional learning tool when developing a new teaching strategy. Whenever we introduce potential changes and developments to practice, we always develop our thinking and understanding through peer learning. Examples include: development of AfL strategies; guided reading; enquiry in science; talk for learning; metacognitive questioning. Peer learning enables teachers to experiment with their practice and get feedback in a safe environment. We also use peer learning to develop our understanding of all aspects of leadership. Examples include parental engagement and coaching. When we first introduced coaching, we used trios of teachers with one being the observer. They would observe the process of coaching and provide feedback.

I was very conscious in my first year that I wanted to develop parental feedback. Staff kept their distance from parents and any sign of challenge from parents was viewed negatively. I wanted to demonstrate to staff how to use coaching techniques to engage in dialogue with parents. Every time I was going to have a potentially difficult meeting with a parent, I would always invite other key staff to observe. We would discuss the meeting and then feed back to the rest of the staff. We developed a shared understanding of how to enable parents to feel listened to and how to manage conversations in such a way that the focus was on children's learning.

Here, I focus on the values of peer learning as a professional learning opportunity where peers observe colleagues' lessons. Peer learning enables self-evaluation and development and offers first-hand experience and direct evidence about what happens in other classrooms. It provides a practical and powerful way to support our practice.

Peer learning offers a means by which teachers can deepen their awareness and understanding of the following:

- What goes on in their classrooms
- The impact of their interactions in the classroom
- Their own and their pupils' learning

It enables assessment for learning processes to have an impact on teacher learning; it puts teachers in control of their own professional learning, allowing them to 'start from where they are'. Peer learning encourages professional dialogue with a particular focus on pupil learning, and helps teachers to develop a 'shared language' about learning and teaching. This is pivotal in developing shared expectations for learning and teaching and for developing consistency of practice across the school.

One example of this occurred when we were first developing talk for learning. Through peer learning observations, we discovered that too often teachers were dominating the discussions in classes and not allowing children to build on each other's ideas. Teachers were intervening and responding to every comment made by the children because this was what they had been used to. We discovered that one powerful strategy for feedback was to give more thinking time to the children. All children were given more time to think about the teacher's questions, reducing the risk of a few children dominating each discussion because of the speed of their responses. Thinking time quickly became embedded across the school. This was a direct result of us visiting each other's classrooms and then engaging in dialogue, leading to established practice across the school.

Peer learning benefits both the observer and the observed, when undertaken in a spirit of collaboration and mutual learning. No judgements are made. The observer has the opportunity to watch and enhance their understanding of the complex interactions taking place in the classroom. They can analyse the relationship between our espoused values (what we say we do) and those theories in action (what actually happens). Peer learning enables the observer to observe in a structured way how a teacher uses different strategies when teaching and the consequent impact on the children. The observer can connect the knowledge and understanding discussed in the preceding PLMs with the practice they see in the classrooms. Ideally, the observers internalise some of the strategies they are observing, embedding these in their own practice. In expansive learning environments in other workplaces, workers regularly get opportunities to observe and question others' practice in a culture of trust and challenge. This can work equally well in the thinking school to secure continual improvement.

The peer being observed also benefits. Many of the countless decisions we make each day are influenced by unconscious thinking and our tacit knowledge, by our own perceptions and understandings of all the experience we have gained in classrooms. The value of peer learning is in providing a reflective lens on our actions in the classroom. When I observe a lesson, I like to give a narrative on what I saw, without judgement. This is itself a learning tool for the teacher, providing an entirely new angle of reflection. I follow up my narrative with certain coaching questions to enable teachers to come to a deeper understanding of what they are doing in their classroom and why, and how this affects the children's learning. Peer learning enables the observed teacher to unpack the complexity of all the interactions that take place in the classroom, in order to learn from their own effective practice to inform future practice.

When I first came to the school, I found it a challenge to move leaders away from the view of lesson observations where feedback was given to the teacher as a series of targets for improvement. To do this in the spirit of peer learning, I asked an NQT if she would be happy for me to observe her teaching and feed back to her at the end of the day in front of the rest of the staff at a professional meeting. This must have been a daunting prospect for her but I wanted to demonstrate how peer learning is undertaken in a safe environment and through structured dialogue about what we saw in the classroom. She taught an English lesson in which children were working in mixed attaining groups on a piece of writing, and then had to share their writing with the class. She demonstrated excellent relationships with the children and we had decided to focus on the extent to which all children were engaged. Examples of the types of coaching questions related to children's engagement that I asked her during this conversation included:

- What would you have liked to see happen that didn't happen?
- What did you do that you think was successful? How well do you think the children were engaged today?

- How do you think these three children engaged in comparison to how they usually are?
- Why did you choose that child to answer that particular question?
- What do you think are the next two things you are going to have to do in this topic? How will you know you have been successful?
- What did you enjoy today and why? How did you feel being observed in this way?

The job of the peer is to question and prompt their colleague to consider their interactions in the classroom and the impact upon the children's learning.

Peer learning is most effective when the focus is on an agreed, specific aspect of practice, and not too general. For examples, specific foci we have used include: metacognitive questioning techniques and engaging children; building ideas within a specific guided reading group; engaging one particular group of children in the class; a good balance of dialogue between adults and children. Peer learning is particularly helpful when teachers are experimenting with and developing new strategies in the classroom. Recently, we have been investigating a new model for teaching scientific enquiry. We use peer learning as a tool to link knowledge and practice, as well as our espoused theories and theories in action. Feedback is an opportunity for professional dialogue where participants explore aspects of the lesson. It is characterised by open questions, where participants collectively evaluate and interpret the evidence collected.

Peers can thus question one another about aspects of the lesson in an open dialogue, with no judgement. It is the difference between mentoring and coaching. As a mentor, we would give advice as to what we think the teacher should have done and this is perfectly appropriate as teachers are developing their experience. In coaching through peer learning, we are questioning the teacher to enable them to come to their own enhanced understanding. In the example of developing scientific enquiry, we are looking at the extent to which children are asking scientific questions. A question for the teacher would be to consider the extent to which their actions during the lesson enabled children to do that. The dialogue enables each peer to develop a deeper awareness of how to teach children the skills of scientific enquiry.

To make peer learning as effective as possible, we learned that we had to ensure that specific factors were in place. Everyone had to be prepared well, in advance of the learning observations. Ideally, peers go into each other's classrooms with a clear and communicated focus. In our three-form entry school, we often operate in groups of three, with two teachers going into each colleague's classroom. The peers need to agree in advance a clear and manageable focus on the specific aspect of practice to be observed. This will usually not involve observing a whole lesson but rather a particular part or aspect of the lesson, such as the whole-class teaching or the group work. Everyone can then remain focused on the key area for development.

Have an agreed pro forma for recording the shared goals of the learning observation to enable you to maintain the agreed structures. This is particularly important in the beginning when you are establishing the process. Some teachers found it difficult to adjust to a different type of lesson observation – particularly some more experienced practitioners. It's challenging when you move away from a hierarchical approach to a peer approach. In peer learning, a headteacher and NQT can be paired together, and it's critical that they see each other as equal peers in the process.

As it's become embedded at our school, it's now a far more natural process and teachers volunteer to arrange and engage in peer learning outside of formally designed CPL learning opportunities identified on the school learning plan. On the pro forma, we had agreed ground rules. This is important in the initial stages for participants to develop high trust in each other. Examples include breaking down exactly what the observer will be doing even to the extent of where they will be sitting and which children they will focus on. We were very keen for teachers to move away from this focus on a showcase lesson, where teachers show off their strengths, and move towards investigating the more complex, tricky aspects of practice. If the observer sees an aspect of practice in the classroom that they feel could be developed – such as quality of classroom displays or use of resources – the matter would not be discussed afterwards because it is not the focus of the professional learning activity. Peer learning has to be seen as an opportunity to experiment and take risks, so both parties should forget hierarchy and focus on providing and receiving professional learning.

Ensure that you arrange the best possible time for the learning observation as well as the best time for the subsequent professional learning conversation, which should take place as soon as possible while it is fresh in participants' minds. Set the time for the lesson observation so as to maximise the learning opportunity for the teacher being observed. The professional learning conversation is designed to prompt thinking between the participants, particularly for the teacher being observed, who can explore their practice in an exceptional way. The peers can explore the agreed aspects of practice that were observed – and the impact on children's learning. The observed teacher has an evidence base from which to arrive at new strategies and actions to trial and implement to enhance their practice even further.

We find it important to emphasise that the observation is a developmental learning opportunity for teachers and not about performance management. It starts from where the teacher is in their learning, enables them to self-assess and come up with their own targets. They can then challenge them through a collaborative dialogue with a trusted peer so they learn within their proximal zone of development to improve their knowledge about teaching and learning and their practice. The longer you practise it in your school, the more embedded it becomes, and the more powerful it is as a professional learning experience for all staff. We engage all staff, not just teachers, in peer learning opportunities.

Sharing peer learning observations through wider professional learning conversations in the school enhances the learning and practice of all the staff. We encountered situations where findings from one peer learning observation led all staff to question their practice at our school. For example, one teacher discovered that they were over-praising a particular child – with the result that the child wasn't sufficiently challenged. Then we all considered our own practice and whether we tended to praise the lower attainers for mediocre progress, and what that meant for the level of challenge for such children.

In another example, we found our responses and questioning with children were leading them to look for the answer they thought was in the teacher's head. This was contrary to our espoused theory of dialogic teaching, so we thought about how effective it would be if we simply didn't comment at all. We found that the dialogic learning exchanges with and between the children improved, confirming the value of high challenge and high trust in the peer learning relationship. This enabled children to build on the ideas of each other rather than just saying what they thought the teacher wanted to hear. The learning that comes from such activities is shared to prompt thinking and develop practice amongst the learning community within the school. This requires the development of high trust between the peer learning participants. The culture of high trust has to be replicated across the school, and takes time to nurture and develop. Aspects of practice that are identified as a potential area for whole-school improvement can then be examined in greater detail. Our findings have led to further whole-school research projects for teachers to pursue.

Chapter 5 describes how we developed all members of staff as coaches. The peer(s) observing lessons must have the opportunity to ask coaching questions, such as: 'How could you have done that better?'; 'What do you think would happen if _____?'; 'What would you do differently next time?'. An authentic coaching relationship enables teachers to focus on the key aspects of practice that need developing. Peer learning enables teachers to take risks, so go in with the belief that the greater the challenge, the greater the learning possibilities. I remember a conversation I had with one teacher when we were first engaging in peer learning. He said he had two lessons prepared: one was fairly safe; the other was more risky, with different groupings of children and open-ended tasks. I told him to go for the second one because, successful or not, he had more to learn from it and therefore more to gain. As the learning community matures, individual teachers across the school elect to engage in peer learning. It becomes part of the toolbox of professional learning activities from which teachers can select in order to develop creative solutions for enhancing pupil outcomes. It is at this point in your development that the teachers will most benefit from engaging in lesson study as a professional learning activity.

Lesson study

Once we had established peer learning as a key teacher learning opportunity at the school, we wanted to go further. As a leadership team, we decided to look for strategies to gain a deeper understanding of our teaching and interactions in the classroom, and the resultant impact on children's learning. We wanted to explore the cycle of teaching at the school, from the initial assessment and planning stages through to the execution of classroom teaching, feedback and marking, and eventually through to children's voice and the impact on their learning. In this section, I will give you a brief introduction to how we organised and implemented it and an example of its impact at our school.

Lesson study has been an established professional development model in Japan for over a century. During my doctoral research, I came across journal articles on lesson study and was fascinated by the concept of this group approach to learning. I was particularly attracted to the learning potential of groups of teachers observing and critically analysing one specific lesson, because it seemed so different from the lesson observations that I had experienced through my career. The thought of being observed by a single person had felt traumatic to colleagues of mine, and I could imagine they would surely be horrified by the idea of being observed by an entire group!

The objective of lesson study is for a group of teachers to observe the delivery of a collaboratively planned lesson, in particular the interactions between the teacher and the children. The group come together as soon as possible after the lesson to analyse and evaluate the outcomes. Ideally, the results are reported back to the school to inform and develop whole-school practice. When we came to introduce lesson study to our school, we were really interested in the entire learning process. We define lesson study as a collaborative professional learning activity where a group of teachers work together to discuss specific learning goals for a group of children. The learning goals are related to either a whole-school professional learning objective or specifically to an individual teacher's professional learning goal. The group collaboratively plan an actual lesson in the classroom; we call this the 'research lesson'. When it comes to the delivery and observation of the actual lesson, each member of the observing group has a specific, identified role – for example, a specific group of children they will be focusing on.

I am a big fan because I experienced the potential of lesson studies when I took part in one during the academic year 2015/16. This was the first year in which our Year 6 children were to be assessed on the revised curriculum for English and maths, meaning that the children would have far tougher end-of-year national tests (SATs). We realised that in maths, for example, we were to be required to teach certain topics (such as fractions) to children at a level that we had had no prior experience of teaching. There were five of us in our research group: me, my deputy and three Year 6 teachers. At the time, each of us was responsible for teaching maths to our own group of children. We decided to plan a lesson collaboratively on the teaching of fractions and invited the least confident person in the group to teach it. Implementing lesson study requires a significant investment of time but, as with many expansive professional learning activities, that investment during the school day paid large dividends in terms of teacher growth and efficacy.

We spent half a day together to plan the lesson. We began by sharing our prior life and work experiences of learning and teaching maths, and particularly fractions. Clearly this can only work within a group where trust is high and there is a shared commitment to learning and growth. We had to address any misconceptions and identify what we believed to be the clear steps in progression for our children's learning. This intense and cathartic process really enabled us to develop our knowledge and understanding. The impact of this formal professional learning opportunity was also felt informally. Over the next few days, we kept gravitating towards each other to discuss aspects of our learning and the development of our thinking about teaching maths. We all felt excited about lesson study, although the teacher being observed admitted to being nervous! However, if teachers experience lesson study in the early stages of their careers, they quickly become comfortable with it.

We were assigned different groups of children to focus on and the four observers watched the teacher deliver the lesson. Afterwards we met as a group to dissect the lesson and share our observations, particularly of the teacher's interactions and interventions with the children to develop their understanding of fractions. We considered the outcome of the lesson that we planned together. This included strategies for teaching the multiplication and division of fractions with different denominators. We realised that the children needed more time to develop a conceptual understanding of fractions and how to find common denominators. They also needed more opportunities to describe the methods they were using. We also commented on the fact that the teacher could have continued to pursue a line of questioning with a child who was unsure – she'd left him and moved on to another child. We felt that challenging the child to think further may have resulted in a better learning outcome.

As a result of our discussion we all decided to change how we taught fractions. So there was an immediate impact on our practice but our engagement in lesson study affected far more than our practice. The lesson study took place in the autumn term and we maintained the professional learning momentum all through that year. Trust among the group was high and we continued our informal and formal professional dialogue around what we were teaching in maths and what the children learned. We developed our teaching of every topic in maths, and this had a dramatic effect on the children's learning during a very challenging year for them. Our learning discussions moved beyond maths, to considering the personal, social and academic development of the children in each subject. When we received question-level analysis of our children's attainment in maths at the end of the year, we found that on average the children performed above national standards in all topics of maths. However, there was one topic in which they performed significantly above the average child in England – fractions!

Sharing our experiences with the rest of the staff at the school promoted a positive attitude to lesson study and formal and informal professional dialogue amongst the staff. We have steadily developed maths teaching practices in line with what we discovered from this lesson study. The teaching of fractions from Year 2 up to Year 6 notably enhanced the children's learning outcomes. 90% of those children in Year 6 achieved the expected standard in maths, in comparison to 70% of children nationally. By 2016/17, that figure had risen to 97%. Only eight schools of a similar or bigger size to ours achieved a higher percentage. So you can see why I'm a fan of lesson study!

Lesson study has developed at the school to the point where I have been observed teaching my maths group by 60 education professionals from Oslo. It takes time to develop the professional learning structures and cultures within the school and the staff team before lesson study can have such a strong impact. We ensure all teachers engage in lesson study and it enables staff to critically challenge each other to improve practice.

Embedding assessment for learning (AfL) and talk for learning (TfL)

The purpose of professional learning is to develop teacher confidence and enhance practice. So the topics the teachers learn about must be focused to that end – to understand the craft of teaching and how their interactions in the classroom impact on children's learning. The two most important areas of practice for teachers to explore and develop are AfL and TfL. AfL and TfL will develop the teachers' passion for engagement in learning. They are inextricably linked to our belief that children's learning is at the centre of everything we do in the thinking school. The success of AfL depends on children's talk. Only by listening to children and understanding their thinking can we determine where they are in their learning and challenge them to move forward.

Assessment for learning

About 15 years ago, I attended a conference on AfL. I sat on the front row as usual and, in line with the first task, I shared my own definition of AfL with the person beside me. I told him that I thought AfL was about teachers identifying where a child is in their learning and challenging them effectively to move them on. This prompted a conversation about the value of AfL and its impact on schools in England at the time. He felt AfL had the potential to transform conceptions of teaching and learning in schools, but cautioned that in 80% of schools it had been misinterpreted and implemented badly. He maintained that the principles of AfL had been misunderstood and that school leaders were using AfL strategies as a checklist of activities for teachers to use in the classroom.

I found out later that my neighbour was Professor Paul Black, co-author of *Inside the Black Box: Raising Standards Through Classroom Assessment*

(Black and Wiliam, 1998). He and Dylan Wiliam reconceptualised the role of formative assessment in raising standards of achievement. Professor Black told me how he believed AfL should be introduced into schools, and stressed that what was needed was 'quality change'. If we wanted quality change of practice in schools, we had to give teachers the space to investigate and experiment over time so they could continually develop and improve their practice. I was already passionate about the value of teacher CPL and that day I added a passion for the powerful combination of CPL and AfL in developing teachers' understanding of their craft, and how to foster children's achievement. I therefore saw my first job at my current school as using CPL – and particularly action research – for the teachers to explore assessment for learning strategies.

When I arrived at the school, most teachers thought they understood and were effectively utilising AfL strategies. I explained that AfL was an area of practice that we could always learn more about and that I was continually experimenting with and developing AfL strategies in my own practice. When we began our professional learning meetings I shared my personal perspective from my own teaching at the school. In that first term, each year group worked in collaborative learning teams to investigate an identified area of AfL practice related to their individual cohorts. Teachers were given access to relevant research, starting from the work of Black and Wiliam, to plan an action research study to evaluate the impact of AfL strategies on children's learning. The research gave them a deeper understanding of authentic AfL strategies and how they influence learning.

The teachers valued their opportunity to engage in peer learning evaluations to assess the impact of their strategies and to inform practice. The peer learning offered an AfL activity for the teachers, putting them in control of their professional learning, starting from where they were in their learning development. The findings from the collaborative learning undertaken by each year group were then collated so we could define what we collectively wanted teaching and learning at the school to look like. We came up with ten guiding principles that we firmly believed should inform our future practice, and I have detailed them below. All staff have to consistently adhere to these principles and we promote and model them in our practice.

1. Give the children confidence and opportunities to ask questions.

Talk is one essential tool of teaching. Children need to talk and to experience a rich menu of spoken language in order to think and learn. Language development is an integral part of learners' cognitive development. We want children to be talking about their learning and asking lots of questions.

We implemented this principle by moving away from the traditional model of question-answer-response exchange that takes place in classrooms. We have a 'no hands up' policy and children are aware they can be called on to answer a question or to share their thoughts at any time. The learning environment values the asking of questions as much as the answering, and we value all responses.

2. Continually adjust the teaching provided in accordance with the results of assessment. Start from what children already know.

Assessments indicate where our children are in their learning and we continually adjust our planning and teaching so we provide sufficient challenge to move them forward.

We always plan and assess collaboratively to enable us to understand how well the children are learning. Regular pupil progress reviews ensure that we adapt our planning to personalise our teaching for the children. These discussions will focus on every possible aspect of each child's learning and development. This ensures that we are always flexible in our provision and that all children make good progress.

3. Give children opportunities to set targets for themselves, to take responsibility for their learning and to evaluate their own progress.

As the children progress through the school, give them increasing opportunities to set targets for themselves and understand what they need to do to improve. Children need to be given opportunities to evaluate their successes against clear criteria. They are then able to identify the improvements they can make to their work.

Our action research project on marking and feedback demonstrated that children were not always responding to teacher's comments, or that teachers were not responding to children's comments. We decided to focus more on verbal feedback, and to give the children more opportunities to self-evaluate. Children are given regular opportunities to mark their own and others' work against clear success criteria. They really enjoy this and are able to describe their own successes and targets – the basis of independent learning.

4. Provide opportunities for children to practise, develop and refine their skills.

Help children to understand the key areas that they need to develop and give them opportunities to practise and improve the skills that support their continual improvement. Practising their skills will enhance their deeper understanding.

We realised that a lot of the learning was taking place for the children at a shallow level, and children had insufficient opportunities to practise those skills – we were moving them on in topics before many of the children had developed a deeper understanding. Children enjoy repeating tasks, for example reading the same book in Early Years or playing the same computer game again and again at home. They know that if they continually practise something, they will improve. We accept this for other areas of learning, such as music, sports or drama, and wanted to transfer this to topics such as maths. When children complete a topic in number, for example division, and move on to handling data, we use the first ten minutes of each lesson for them to build on and practise the division skills they were learning over the previous two weeks. This enables them to practise and refine the skills they have learned over a longer period – we would also not move them on in their division learning until they have had sufficient time to practise. To do this well, teachers need excellent subject knowledge – the CPL activities in the thinking school are designed to develop this.

5. Listen actively to children and give them effective feedback.

The feedback relates directly to the learning intentions and success criteria and is based on teachers' understanding of each child and of their particular learning needs and current development. By listening to children, teachers understand their current learning and can provide focused feedback that supports their progress.

To develop this principle, every teacher was observed working with a group of children and the dialogue was recorded and transcribed. A professional learning meeting was used to evaluate the transcript, particularly in terms of how each teacher was building on the responses of children. We found we needed to improve the quality of our listening – to think more deeply about the children's responses to enable a better understanding of them as learners. We found we were correcting responses, when we could have repeated the response to allow the child to self-correct. Developing all staff as coaches also improved our active listening skills.

6. Set clear learning objectives and success criteria and set out how the lesson fits within the child's learning journey.

Ensure that children understand what they are learning and why. We ensure that our learning intentions are clear, and don't confuse the children with the context. Involve children in their learning by stating, and establishing with them, success criteria:

- *Learning intentions tell us **what** we are going to learn.*
- *Activities determine **how** we will learn.*
- *Success criteria tell us **how** we will know if we have succeeded.*

We reflect upon learning and teaching to assess whether the learning intentions have been realised and whether the context suited all the children. Ask the following questions of the learning activity in order to determine the success:

- *How will you tell whether the product you create is good?*
- *How will you tell if the process you adopt is good?*
- *How do you intend to do the best you can in this learning?*

Through our ongoing research, we continually evaluate our AfL strategies to ensure they are effective and meeting the needs of all children. We work together to plan the best way to set success criteria and learning intentions. Engage your staff in dialogue to ensure that the policies are meeting the children's needs. We now feel that the three questions above provide effective starting points to enable children to understand what they are learning and why, and how they will self-evaluate. Teachers are now asked to consider these questions for themselves when they are collaboratively planning learning activities.

7. Include time for paired and group discussions and plan for opportunities to summarise and link learning through mini-reviews.

Children have to work collaboratively and learn from each other. Mini-reviews afford opportunities for teachers to summarise and link learning for individuals, groups, and the class as a whole.

To reinforce this principle, we compiled a set of criteria for excellent AfL practice for all staff. The criteria included an agreement for teachers to ensure that all lessons incorporated opportunities for children to engage in paired and group discussions. Consistency comes from modelling and valuing this type of engagement when we visit classrooms.

Emphasise the role of the teacher in summarising the learning for children – examples include:

- The teacher articulating to the entire class how far a group of children have improved in their learning during a topic, e.g. 'This group were really struggling to come up with ideas for their persuasive letter to the council. But look at this sheet of paper, where they shared their ideas for different questions they could ask. Look at all that powerful thinking. How did you get these ideas? They then put each question at the start of a paragraph. I think their letter is really persuasive because _____. What do you think?'

- Articulating to all children the improvement of one particular child, e.g. 'Wow, Alexia! I can't believe you just did that. Remember when Alexia was finding it really difficult to understand how to add fractions with different denominators? She's been really thinking and practising hard, and she's been asking me lots of questions. She kept getting it wrong but she didn't give up. Why don't you come up to the front and share your method with the class. Fantastic, I think I'm going to call it the Alexia method. I'm going to use this method too now.'

8. Use a range of questioning strategies to ensure that all the children are engaged in learning throughout the lesson.

Questioning is at the heart of learning and teaching. Lessons must afford rich and varied questions and opportunities to talk. They are built in in the following ways:

- *Giving children extended time to think before answering*
- *Selecting the children who answer – no hands up*
- *Encouraging children to consult with their group or partner in order to formulate their answers*
- *Involving several children in responding to a single question, creating the opportunity for discussion – e.g. asking 'What do you think?'; 'Do you agree with that answer?'*
- *Putting wrong answers to use to develop the child's understanding*
- *Employing good question stems – e.g. 'Why does…?'; 'What if…?'; 'How would you…?'; 'Could you explain…?'*
- *Affording opportunities for pupils to formulate questions*
- *Using mini whiteboards for children to write their thoughts and ideas*

Implement this principle by giving these strategies to staff and ask them to experiment with them in their classrooms. As a team, these strategies were formulated from our research. Our guiding principles are provided to each staff member in a 'Highlands Learning Journal' that is given at the beginning of each academic year. This reminds staff of our agreed practices. It is then up to us all, when we visit each other's classrooms, to use them as guidance for the professional learning conversations that follow. I find them particularly useful when I am presenting model lessons to groups of visitors from abroad. My visits to schools in Oslo have shown that these strategies are not reflected in classrooms there – you are more likely to see traditional models of teacher-pupil questioning and children working independently from textbooks.

9. Provide opportunities for peer and self-assessment/evaluation.

Children need regular opportunities to assess their own work, and that of others. Give them opportunities to engage in self-reflection and to identify the next steps in their learning. By engaging in self-assessment, self-evaluation and reflection, the learners take growing responsibility for – and ownership of – their learning. They begin to develop an understanding of themselves as individual learners. Peer assessment and evaluation needs to be conducted with an ethos of respect for every learner.

We implemented this principle by ensuring that children were clear about the success criteria for a task before beginning it. This meant that they were more likely to be self-evaluating during the process of the task. We also give them opportunities to edit their work and self-assess to improve it. Give lots of opportunities for children to peer assess and then feed back their evaluations to the class. This develops a whole-class understanding of effective assessment, lessening the need for an adult to assess. We want our children to be independent in their learning and less reliant on adults. In classrooms where there are poor levels of AfL, children become more reliant on the teacher and the gap between higher and lower attainers will grow.

10. Afford learners the opportunity to acknowledge their successes and give them time to work on improving their learning outcomes.

Children need to be given the time to make improvements to their work and learning.

We found that it was better to give additional time for children to work on one task in depth rather than complete several tasks. Ensure that you give several opportunities for children to improve their work – this enables them to consider each task and their own learning in greater detail. Creativity comes from successive failures, and the more opportunities we get to refine and improve our work, the better.

I see little difference between what comprises a positive learning experience for children and a positive learning experience for adults. So we could easily apply these ten guiding principles to our teacher learning too.

Talk for Learning

At the same time that I was developing a passion for assessment for learning, I had begun to explore the concept of talk for learning. My initial introduction was through Robin Alexander's seminal work on dialogic teaching. I was fascinated by his framework for dialogic teaching in harnessing the power of talk to stimulate and promote children's thinking, learning and understanding. Within the thinking school, children's talk is as important as teachers' talk – or more so – as we believe that all learning happens through talk. This is particularly significant in a school such as ours with a high proportion of children with English as an additional language. However, we find that enabling a learning environment in the classroom in which children's talk is central will benefit all children. My entire first term was spent developing our understanding of AfL through the CPL strategies I've described. In the second term, we replicated the model and investigated our understanding and practice of talk for learning.

If we improved the quality of talk, I said, we could improve the quality of learning and the children's attainment. We actively promoted children's awareness of talk as a tool for thinking, emphasising the value of both teacher talk and pupil talk. Our vision was to ensure that classroom talk moved away from the traditional question-answer responses and embraced an extended pattern of thinking where teachers used questioning to guide the development of children's understanding. We wanted to ensure that our curriculum was not focused solely on developing children's subject knowledge, but that their learning took place at a deeper level where children could solve problems, make sense of their experiences and see learning as a social activity.

The professional learning focus for the term was therefore talk for learning. It began with a day in which the teachers and children were not allowed to write at all. No written recordings or resources were allowed, only dialogue for them to discuss their findings and explain their thinking. The purpose was to enable teachers and children to reflect upon the value of talk and compare the quality of learning with that in a normal day at school. At the end of the day we held a PLM to share our experiences, and had a shared reading session on Robin Alexander's (2017) work on dialogic talk. We considered what we were working towards and how we could build a vision for our future practice.

As with our approach to AfL, we engaged in peer learning activities and each year group team established a research project to develop their understanding of talk for learning. Teachers had the opportunity during the term to explore metacognition and the ways effective questioning might generate talk and reasoning amongst children. One particularly powerful learning activity was analysing transcripts of learning conversations with children to explore how the quality of dialogue had developed, and how teachers could ask the children authentic questions. In a reflective learning activity, pairs of teachers evaluated a transcribed session of dialogue from their own teaching, judging whether their learning environments were enabling a positive climate for exploratory talk, thus reflecting upon their practice from a fresh perspective.

Teachers discussed their transcripts in a PLM and shared their experiences. We were able to unpick certain key themes that were emerging from our practice. We found that our interactions often led to children looking for the answer they thought was in their teacher's head, rather than sharing their own thoughts. We also found that we often intervened too often and too soon. We needed to give children time to share their thoughts and build on the responses of other children. Essentially, we needed to let children lead their talk and learning; our job was to facilitate opportunities for quality talk. It was often better to say nothing. It was a difficult transition for teachers to leave extended pauses and allow time for the children to think and build on their own and others' responses – as teachers it can seem natural to us to respond immediately to every comment in the classroom.

Following the investigative work in our classrooms, we identified ten guiding principles to inform our future practice. Identifying principles is important in the thinking school. It crystallises our thinking and clarifies the key learning outcomes from our CPL activities. It gives us a reference point to return to in the future, to remind us of why we do what we do and to re-evaluate our practice in relation to the principles. It also serves as a useful starting point for new practitioners coming to the school. And it enables us to maintain good practice. During my career, I have witnessed the positive impact of strategies that have been imposed on schools slowly dissipate as practitioners return to their former practices. When practitioners are allowed to investigate their own practice and make changes accordingly, the impact is greater and sustained. Guiding principles for talk:

1. Ask children how they feel about their learning.

How often do we ask our children how they feel about their learning? What do they enjoy? What are they excited about? What do they find challenging? Children's responses help us to tune into their minds, how they think and what they do and don't know. Regular reflection points in lessons will support children's progress.

We implemented this principle by giving each teacher a list of metacognitive questions and asking them to consider which questions they regularly used in their questioning and which they didn't. The questions were organised into three groups: metacognitive knowledge, metacognitive skills and metacognitive beliefs. Metacognitive questions are designed to develop children's higher-order thinking skills. They enable children to think about and discuss their thinking and learning. Examples of metacognitive knowledge questions include: 'What can you do today that you couldn't do yesterday?'; 'What did you say to yourself in your head?' Metacognitive skills questions are questions like: 'Why did you choose to do it in that way?'; 'What do you think you still need help with?'

We found that the area that was least utilised by teachers was metacognitive beliefs – the teachers that said they did use them regularly were immediately recognised by colleagues as being particularly nurturing. These teachers maintained excellent relationships with all children, but particularly those with emotional and behavioural needs. Examples of metacognitive belief questions include:

- What were you proud of today?
- Why do you enjoy doing that?
- How do you feel when you learn something new?
- What did you do to make sure you got the right answer?

2. Use effective questioning techniques and encourage children to ask questions that further their learning.

Ask open-ended questions that have more than one possible answer. Open-ended questions deepen the children's understanding and require them to reflect. We need to break away from teachers' addiction to the 'right answer' and from children trying to guess what it is. Productive questions include conversation starters such as:

- What do you think?
- Why do you think that?
- How do you know?
- Do you have a reason?
- Can you be sure?
- Is there another way?

Continually referring to these types of questions and reflecting upon our own practice enables us to develop their use, and they become embedded as part of daily practice. Peer learning and lesson study will reinforce our commitment to this.

3. Promote an even balance of talk by teachers and children in class.

In any learning encounter neither the teacher nor the child is passive. In a true dialogic classroom, children engage and teachers actively and constructively intervene.

We used the TfL research projects to self-evaluate our interactions in the classroom, and the balance of teacher and children talk. When teachers discussed their learning at professional meetings, they shared the value of extending the dialogue by asking children to give their opinions on the responses of others. This meant that children built on each other's ideas rather than waiting for the teacher to respond to the comment of every child.

4. Encourage children to speak in complete sentences and to use precise and elaborated language.

Children need to talk and to experience a varied diet of spoken language to support them in their thinking. Talk is the foundation of learning. We tend to pay less attention to children's talk than their written work. Be sure to model the use of formal language and expect the children to express their own thinking.

We use our own PLMs to model expectations of language. The master's-level learning sessions ensure that we hold high expectations for our own learning. We want our children to be able to compete in the job market with children from more-privileged backgrounds – we want to give them the language to do that. We constantly promote the value of high expectations for our children's language development.

5. Establish high expectations of talk and dialogue in the classroom through talk charters.

At the beginning of the year, open up discussions with the children about why they feel talk is important to their learning. What skills demonstrate excellent talk and dialogue? Children are given interactive activities to engage in talk so they can identify the skills by which they succeed in their tasks. The key findings from the children are put on display and regularly referred to in teaching and learning to emphasise high expectations of talk and dialogue in the classroom.

It is not as simple as giving opportunities for children to talk in class. We realised that we needed to teach children the skills to talk well – for example, how to wait for your turn to speak, and how to respond to a comment you may disagree with. The talk charter represents the agreed class rules for quality talk. Right from the Early Years the children are taught to engage in group talk and build on these skills each year. Visitors to our school are always impressed with the quality of both pupil talk and engagement.

6. Be aware of the risk of scaffolding too much, lest less active children become 'experts' in seeking help.

Children need the opportunity to explore and discover new learning for themselves. They need time to think things through rather than the boundaries of scaffolding and prompting. It is too easy for passive learners to rely on a scaffold or teacher support to help find answers rather than taking ownership of their learning. Allow pupils to think for themselves how they could solve a problem or what resources they could access to support their understanding.

Our research found that we were too quick in scaffolding the learning for children, particularly for those that may have been struggling. When children are given further opportunities to consider the problem themselves, they take risks and become more resilient. We also found that most teachers stop at the right answer. By that, I mean that we often ask a question and take as many responses as we can until we come to the right answer. We found that we didn't need to do that and we could continue taking as many responses as possible. This meant that more children were engaged, more got the opportunity to respond and there was additional time available for children to self-assess and self-correct.

7. Understand the power of teaching from children's misconceptions and allowing them to talk through the processes of identifying these misconceptions.

Children need to identify any misconceptions they form in their learning and they should be given an opportunity to think and talk it through so that they can articulate their own journey to understanding a key concept. Take time to pick up on misconceptions with both the individual and the class, as other children may have similar misconceptions. We need to ensure this is within a climate where all pupils feel safe to make mistakes and develop from these.

We realised the value of learning from mistakes and misconceptions when we engaged in peer learning activities. We then shared this finding with the staff team and encouraged teams of teachers to consider how to incorporate misconceptions and mistakes when planning. Often, children are given opportunities to mark anonymised pieces of writing or a page of sums. They are then asked to identify the misconceptions made, thereby strengthening their own subject knowledge. It is the difference between being told something and discovering it for yourself – the creative process in self-assessing and learning from misconceptions will lead to deeper and more sustainable learning.

8. Model thoughts out loud to encourage higher-order thinking skills.

Children need to be provided with models of language and critical thinking skills. Children especially benefit from the modelling of inter-thinking between adults in the classroom.

We found that the children really benefited from listening to the adults' thinking processes and learning strategies. We encourage all teachers to undertake every activity that the children are asked to complete, for example a poster or a maths test. The teacher can then discuss how they approached the task and share strategies they used to be as successful as possible. They can also share the challenges they faced and what they found difficult. This encourages more children to share their own thinking. Children love to see the work that the teacher has produced.

9. Provide developmental oral feedback to extend children's thinking further.

Ensure that feedback to children is encouraging, informs thinking and leads it forward. Be specific about why a child's response was well thought out, how it could be further enhanced, what further links might be made, where the viewpoints come from, how the children know something, and linking their responses to the next steps in learning.

We found that we were giving too much shallow feedback that did not move children's learning on, for example saying 'Well done!' and 'Excellent!' without giving the child a clear explanation of what they had done well and why it was useful to learning. We had a whole-school focus on evaluative praise, making it clear when praising what it was that the child had done well and how this was linked to their learning.

10. Ensure that the classroom space is used so as to be conducive to talk.

Make optimal use of the space in classrooms and elsewhere in the school to facilitate opportunities for high-quality talk. Remove barriers between teachers and children, re-arranging furniture to allow for circle time sessions and drama, use halls and specialist group rooms for interaction.

We found during our research modules on pedagogy and creativity that our learning space in the classroom in particular needed to be more flexible in facilitating children's talk. Each year group team looked to rearrange their classroom spaces in a way that the teacher could quickly move from whole-class teaching to paired work to group work to independent work in a way that optimised children's learning experiences.

Summary

We have looked at two key activities that support teacher professional learning and two key topics that underpin children's learning. This chapter is informed by my own experiences of implementing teacher action research and peer learning/lesson study over my six years as a headteacher. I have tried to show that peer learning and lesson study are valuable collaborative learning tools that facilitate professional dialogue about teaching and learning, and that leaders in schools are crucial to a climate that encourages such activities to flourish and be used in authentic and creative ways. I have similarly shared my passion and enthusiasm for optimising AfL and TfL for teachers and children. I have demonstrated the importance of these strategies in both forming the starting points for teacher professional learning and to develop our children as motivated, committed, self-confident and independent learners.

Relevant reading

Alexander, R. J. (2017) *Towards dialogic teaching: rethinking classroom talk*. 5th edn. York: Dialogos.

Black, P. and Wiliam, D. (1998) *Inside the black box: raising standards through classroom assessment*. London: GL Assessment.

Cordingley, P., Higgins, S., Greany, T., Buckler, N., Coles-Jordan, D., Crisp, B., Saunders, L. and Coe, R. (2015) *Developing great teaching: lessons from the international reviews into effective professional development*. London: Teacher Development Trust.

Elliot, J. (2007) 'Assessing the quality of action research', *Research Papers in Education* 22 (2) pp. 229–246.

General Teaching Council for England (2007) *Making CPD better: bringing together research about CPB*. London: GTCE.

Hoban, G. F. (2002) *Teacher learning for educational change*. Buckingham: Open University Press.

Kraft, M. A. and Papay, J. P. (2014) 'Do supportive professional environments promote teacher development? Explaining heterogeneity in returns to teaching experience', *Educational Evaluation and Policy Analysis* 36 (4) pp. 476–500.

McNiff, J. and Whitehead, J. (2005) *Action research for teachers: a practical guide*. London: David Fulton.

Stenhouse, L. (1975) *An introduction to curriculum research and development*. London: Heinemann.

Reflective questions

1. What opportunities do practitioners in your school have to engage in research?

2. How could you develop further teacher engagement in research?

3. To what extent do teachers at your school have the opportunity to engage in peer learning and lesson study?

4. Is there a shared understanding of assessment for learning practices amongst staff at your school?

5. To what extent is talk for learning practised at your school? Is it something that you would like to develop? How do you feel your staff would respond to it?

Chapter 5

Developing the culture in the thinking school

Why is it so important to develop the culture in the thinking school? We want all our teachers to have positive individual dispositions to learning and a commitment to collaborative learning. The central argument in the thinking school is that through the promotion of specific professional learning activities, like collaborative action research, peer learning and lesson study, we develop a culture for learning and a passion for personal and professional growth. You may be reading this book and imagining colleagues you've worked with that would not be willing to participate in the activities I've described. Within a distributed leadership structure, we are creating a learning environment that promotes a culture of individual and collaborative learning and development. In this chapter, I describe how we strengthen this culture through specifically creating opportunities to model and share practice, as well as opportunities for teachers to work and learn together. To enable all our teachers to become solution-focused, we develop their skills as coaches.

Factors that affect teacher learning in schools

If we are to create an authentic professional learning culture, we first need to examine the factors that affect the quality of teacher professional learning experiences. We saw in chapter 3 that the factors that influence teacher engagement in learning in schools include the expansiveness of the learning environment, individual dispositions to learning, and school leaders. Teacher engagement in collaborative action research is a fundamental element of professional learning for teachers (see chapter 4). Here I draw on findings from my own research to highlight the challenges teachers perceived they faced when engaging in both action research and in wider professional learning activities. Many of the factors that were considered particularly important to the quality of teachers' learning were also considered challenging and were critical to the perceived success. The four major challenges were: time and workload constraints; teacher self-confidence as researchers; individual dispositions and attitudes; leadership support.

Let's take teacher research for example. The potential for teachers to achieve success through engagement in collaborative action research depends on whether they are: given sufficient time during the school day and beyond to engage deeply in research; given the tools and resources to motivate them to engage in research; working in partnership with equally motivated teachers; and supported effectively by school leaders. Thus cultures and structures are inextricably linked. The more often teachers are engaged in effective collaborative action research, the more motivated and self-confident they become as reflective practitioners and researchers. The learning activities enhance the learning culture.

We need to manage our teachers' time in such a way that part of their professional practice involves engagement in action research. Leaders have to demonstrate a commitment to action research by allowing teachers to have the time to research. School leaders who criticise our model of promoting teacher research tell me that their teachers aren't motivated to engage in research or have no time because their school has other priorities. In the thinking school, commitment to teacher research is based on its effectiveness both in professionally developing our teachers and in promoting their wellbeing.

The more teachers become self-confident and knowledgeable in their practice, the more they feel in control of their complex and challenging job. Consequently, they are less likely to feel stressed and develop greater self-efficacy. Give teachers time to reflect upon their practice; cover for their classes as and when required. Then their practice becomes more effective and the children's learning improves. What I am saying is that teacher engagement in action research cannot just be in addition to all their responsibilities.

Learning over time is beneficial. Evidence from my research demonstrates the importance of time both to the action research cycle and to the formation of a successful professional learning community. Leaders and the motivation of teachers were factors found to encourage teachers to engage in research and to form a learning community. A number of previous studies have emphasised the importance of motivating and engaging teachers and of giving them the confidence to view themselves as researchers. This is particularly important when considering the range of teachers within any given school, their previous life and work experiences, and how these things influence teacher motivation to engage in action research or wider professional learning.

Teachers were motivated to conduct research that focused on classroom actions and aspects of teaching and learning. They wanted to be in charge of identifying their research focus. Crucially, they had to be able to identify and understand the value of research as they are not necessarily researchers by trade; they are practitioners. Leaders need to model the skills of researchers and particularly their motivation and commitment. This doesn't mean they have to be experts. It is more important that they demonstrate curiosity and criticality about their own practice and are willing to work collaboratively with teacher colleagues to investigate each other's practice. Openness in professional dialogue and commitment to learning and developing their practice are what counts. When I asked one of our teachers why she was so committed to research, she replied, 'School leaders told me that it made them better teachers and I want that too.'

Leaders in schools have key responsibilities to enable teachers' engagement in action research. Just as teachers encourage children to overcome challenging learning activities, so leaders need to encourage teachers. Teachers rely on their school leaders to promote an institutional culture that underpins the action research. My research found that although teachers thought action research was a good idea, most of them were unwilling to give up their precious teaching time. However, this changed when the headteacher supported them and embedded it in school policy. This section of the book is about strengthening a culture within your school that is conducive to engaging in professional learning. My doctoral study investigated wider potential factors that influence teacher engagement in professional learning.

Key areas to consider include:

- The significant influence of Ofsted in determining school priorities for teachers' professional development
- The importance for teachers of relevant and personalised learning experiences
- The importance of collaborative learning activities

Ofsted has never stipulated in the inspection framework that teachers need to engage in certain types of professional learning activities. However, the inspection framework's emphasis on performativity indirectly encourages school leaders to focus on short-term professional learning activities for teachers. And it discourages active participation in many of the activities promoted in this book. Leaders are often afraid to distribute leadership and empower staff to lead their learning because of a focus on short-term goals in preparation for their next Ofsted inspection.

During my research I was invited to meet with the then Minister of State for Schools, who was particularly interested in our model for teacher learning. He wanted to know about how we retained our staff and engaged so many in master's-level study. His big question was how the model at our school could be replicated across more schools. I spoke to him about Ofsted and how school leaders were operating in a climate of fear – they are focused on the latest government initiative and ensuring that staff are compliant and prepared to demonstrate that they are a 'good' or 'outstanding' school at their next inspection. I explained that until we have an inspection regime that values teacher learning and assesses its quality during an inspection, school leaders are equally unlikely to value it.

The culture of audit-led performance through both Ofsted and local authority leadership has neglected the processes of teacher learning over time. Ball (2012) has discussed how this performativity culture presses schools to focus their efforts on performance rather than experiential learning. League tables and the inspection process have too often ensured that money available to schools has been directed at government priorities and external courses. Leaders in schools need to be brave. The professional learning activities highlighted here promote the long-term growth of teachers and develop their practice. We have shown that a strong emphasis on teacher learning will impact on children's learning, and this success is reflected in league tables. If we adhere to our principles, an inspection will take care of itself. We will demonstrate that we have a team of empowered knowledgeable practitioners capable of enabling children's learning and justifying their own professional intentions and practice.

Most headteachers will work with an associate advisor who provides an external view on the school and its effectiveness. They will visit each half-term to evaluate different areas of practice. In most schools, this will be restricted to a conversation with the headteacher. When I, as a headteacher, visit a classroom and wish to evaluate the effectiveness of the class teacher, I will observe and question the children; similarly, if an associate advisor wants to measure my effectiveness, there's no point in just talking to me – I would expect them to question the staff I lead. Therefore, when our associate advisor visits, I select a random group of staff members for them to interrogate. Every advisor that we have worked with has been very clear in judging our practices to be highly unusual!

The value of collaborative learning

My research confirmed the value of collaborative learning in schools, both formally and informally. Consider the extent to which your environment provides opportunities for teachers to learn collaboratively. Remember that authentic collaboration requires equal participation, with shared values and goals – it's not just about putting people together in a room. I define collaborative learning as the additional opportunities made available to teachers to work together. There are insufficient opportunities for teachers to work collaboratively in many schools, and they are more likely to be developing in isolation. The impact of collaborative learning is also dependent on the individuals involved, and the extent to which they equally value and commit to working with each other.

The key collaborative learning activities I have highlighted in this book include: collaborative action research, peer learning and lesson study, collaborative planning, project work with teachers from different Key Stages, team-teaching, and peer coaching – all within a model of distributed leadership. The thinking school sets out to create a culture in which collaborative learning is seen as the norm and so is therefore highly valued and utilised. Not all teachers will be equally motivated to collaborate. Leaders need to be seen to be equally collaborative and promote and recruit members of staff who demonstrate a commitment to collaborative learning.

Measures such as performance-related pay mean that teachers are more likely to be competing rather than collaborating. During my research, I found examples of teachers being negative, inhibiting colleagues' learning during collaboration. These included less-experienced teachers in year group teams feeling as if they didn't have a voice during planning meetings. Promote a culture where teachers are able to share their worries and concerns about their teaching in a safe environment. Leaders can model this when they participate in planning meetings.

In my first year of headship, I went to observe a highly motivated and reflective teacher in his third year of teaching. He was very animated and energetic during the maths lesson; but unfortunately, the children didn't learn very much. One group in particular were not challenged at all: the activity they were given was too easy for them. When I had a coaching conversation with him afterwards, I asked him what his reasoning was behind the activity set for this group. He explained that he had simply been following the planning he'd been given for that lesson. One of the other teachers in the year group – an experienced teacher and former maths leader – had written the plan for her own class and shared it with her colleagues. He had misinterpreted the task but he hadn't had the confidence to question his colleague. When questioned further, he explained that he often didn't ask questions of his experienced colleagues during the shared planning sessions because he didn't want to be seen to be taking up too much of their time. I also suspect that he didn't feel confident in revealing perceived deficiencies. As teachers, we often feel that we are expected to be the expert in our role.

This is an example of where it looks like teachers are working collaboratively but the culture does not support it. The teacher did not feel confident in sharing his misconceptions or doubts. He is a highly dedicated and motivated professional but wasn't developing his teaching to its full potential. I knew, because of his commitment, that with strong professional learning opportunities, the quality of his teaching would improve rapidly. Within two years, in a collaborative learning culture of action research, peer learning and collaborative planning, he was appointed as the first specialist leader of education (SLE) for reading in the LA and was presenting his work at national conferences. As a newly appointed year group leader, he led his team in a very inclusive and collaborative way. Remember that teachers within each year group see themselves as responsible for all 90 children rather than just their own classes. Team planning sessions are more likely to be collaborative if this is the case.

Take as many opportunities as possible to ensure that teachers have opportunities to work together. This collaboration should involve support staff and colleagues they may not otherwise be working with. Examples include whole-school events such as a drama production, winter fair or sports day. As colleagues work together, a culture for collaborative learning will grow. Avoid restricting responsibilities to individual teachers. Primary schools will traditionally have individual areas of responsibility such as an English subject leader or special educational needs co-ordinator (SENCo). We ensure that as far as possible, areas of responsibility are shared by staff members. We have an Inclusion team, an English team and a Creative Curriculum team. Each year, different people can have leadership responsibilities in each team. This is an example of a structure at our school that promotes a wider collaborative learning culture. Teams of teachers will work together on collaborative action research projects and their findings will inform future practice. To ensure that collaboration is successful, the learning has to be relevant to the individual teacher's needs as well as enabling all participants to have equal input and voice in planning and designing the learning.

The value of modelling and sharing practice

Learning-focused leaders effectively model learning behaviours and skills to their staff. To develop confident, creative and reflective risk-takers in your teams, you have to model and exhibit these learning behaviours and skills. In this section, I detail how the modelling and sharing of practice enables us to co-construct knowledge about teaching practice with our staff. To establish a persistent, public focus on learning and teaching, it is essential that school leaders take every possible opportunity to model their values and core beliefs in their teaching practice. If leaders take opportunities to model teaching and engage in professional dialogue about all matters pertaining to learning and teaching, the effectiveness of teaching and its impact on children's learning outcomes will improve.

Leaders should be viewed as lead learners. Research (Leithwood et al., 2006) has demonstrated that school leadership is second only to classroom teaching as an influence on children's learning. Part of this influence will include leaders engaging in the same learning activities and practice as teachers. This will include the specific modelling of teaching – teaching a lesson that is observed by individual/groups of teachers. Ensure that teachers have a specific focus for this observation, such as: use of questioning; engagement of different groups of children; use of resources; modelling teaching strategies. In addition, leaders will engage in team-teaching, peer learning, lesson study, coaching and collaborative planning alongside teachers.

Remember that modelling of practice and observations of each other's teaching has to be done in a non-judgemental way in a culture of high trust. If all teachers are prepared to model teaching to colleagues, we are sending out the message that the core business of the school is teaching and learning. We are also demonstrating that teaching is not an exact science and that we are constantly improving our practice. In the same way that we want our children to develop metacognitive skills and a passion and independence for learning, we must want the same for our teachers. Through the sharing of practice, we are happy to expose our flaws and take creative risks to learn and improve. We are learning collectively and continually co-constructing knowledge about what we would like learning and teaching to look like at our school. I have often been told by leaders that they have become deskilled as teachers because they have been out of the classroom for so long. This can have a negative impact on their credibility as lead learners. As we collaboratively develop our practice, it is important that we are all engaging in teaching and modelling practice.

In my first year, I took opportunities to model specific aspects of practice. I demonstrated the use of maths resources, such as a counting stick, to develop children's mental maths skills. I also modelled how to use AfL strategies such as 'thinking time' and 'no hands up' to effectively engage all children. These modelled sessions form starting points for discussion with colleagues. It is not about showing off or teaching the perfect lesson. It is about demonstrating strategies as a starting point for professional dialogue. When I was in my second year of teaching, I watched an experienced teacher deliver a maths lesson to my class. It was fascinating to watch her as she engaged and enthused my children with resources and key questioning. It is a valuable learning opportunity to watch how your class react to another adult. It is accepted that as student teachers, we learn from observing and questioning our mentors' teaching. How many opportunities do teachers at your school get to observe their colleagues teaching?

I often go into classes and pick up strategies that teachers are using. The culture within the school has to support this openness and sharing of practice. During my first year as a headteacher, I recall that every time I went to visit one highly experienced teacher, she would feel nervous. She was suspicious of my intentions, and this was a consequence of her previous experiences of leadership. I think she thought that I was checking up on her and judging her. It takes time to build a culture in which all teachers are happy to be observed teaching by colleagues. As leaders, you are constantly modelling to staff. When you are leading a professional learning meeting, the way in which you motivate and engage teachers is the way in which you want those teachers to engage their children. Be inclusive in your approach; every teacher's voice should be heard. You should also be able to challenge colleagues in these meetings, to reflect on each other's practice to continually improve.

When I first arrived at my school, teachers spoke to me about their negative experiences of lesson observations. They had just experienced a difficult Ofsted inspection and were genuinely anxious when being observed, feeling that it was a process that was done *to* them (rather than *with* them or *for* them) and that judgements made of their teaching were inconsistent. Observations had been hierarchical and teachers never had opportunities to observe leaders or even each other. Judgemental lesson observations take up considerable time but do not necessarily lead to a positive learning experience. In the same way that children can focus on grades rather than development points, teachers were interested only in their grading and not the learning opportunities. Therefore, teachers tended to play safe. Traditional lesson observations do not encourage the type of creativity and risk-taking that we wish to encourage and the consequent reflection to support deeper learning.

Against the advice of the local authority advisors, I undertook no formal observations of teaching in my first term as headteacher. I encouraged all teachers to come and watch me teach. Not because I wanted to show them what a good teacher I was; it was to show that I had the same frailties they did but that I was constantly reflecting and willing to engage in dialogue about my practice. I wanted them to understand that lesson observations and the subsequent dialogue could be a positive learning experience for all. Sixteen of the teachers at the school came to observe me teaching. We had begun the process of building a culture of high trust and high challenge. I was modelling what I believe to be the most important core belief in schools: that our learning and teaching across the school has huge impact upon children's personal, social, emotional and academic learning. And I wanted our learning and teaching to be transformational.

Learning and teaching should be established as central topics for all conversations in school, through activities such as modelling and sharing practice. My research revealed that in high-performing schools, school leaders engage in collaborative professional learning with teachers. As a learning-focused leader myself, I regularly visit classrooms and participate in professional learning conversations with staff. These exchanges may then be shared with the wider staff team to model the whole-school emphasis on learning and teaching. School leaders in the thinking school need to be skilled at recognising and creating common ground amongst their teams.

Teachers should have the opportunity to visit classrooms across the school. One particularly powerful learning opportunity took place when Year 6 and Reception teachers engaged in peer learning. Initially, it was simply about providing the opportunity to observe children's learning and teaching in a different year group. The participants were able to establish commonalities across the year groups; for example, evaluating how independent the children were and how many choices the children had in their learning. It gave teachers the opportunity to understand where the learners in our community were coming from and where they were going. And it brought the two year group teams closer together. Learning-focused leaders' direct involvement in observing and discussing practice across the school enables all staff to understand the challenges faced by their colleagues, and how we collectively enable our children to succeed.

PLMs should be used to support collaborative learning and the sharing of practice. Give teachers opportunities to share their findings from lessons that they have observed as well as opportunities to model and share strategies with their colleagues. Last year, we had a specific school focus on developing children's enquiry skills in science. During one PLM, all teachers had the opportunity to engage in a science experiment that was led and modelled by two teachers. By engaging in the activity, we considered our own scientific enquiry skills and how we could develop our teaching to provide more opportunities for children to develop those same skills. We use PLMs to model our values and to share reflections on our observations of learning and teaching in classrooms. PLMs should be utilised as an opportunity for groups of teachers and leaders to engage in learning activities and to co-construct knowledge about learning that informs practice.

In the thinking school, all staff will model learning-focused leadership by talking about learning and teaching. All staff observe each other's teaching and they plan and evaluate each other's teaching to lead learning collaboratively. Within this culture, all staff are learning from each other and teaching each other, regardless of their experience or status. Good leaders lead by example, and when the core business of any school is learning, leading by example involves being the lead learner and modelling the attitudes and dispositions to learning that they wish to develop in their colleagues and children.

The value of coaching

Coaching is a fundamental professional learning activity for all the staff of the thinking school. It supports the development of positive individual dispositions to learning, both as coach and coachee. As an experienced coach myself, it remains the most powerful learning activity that I engage in. Through coaching, individuals become more solution-focused and are able to self-assess and find answers to complex questions. Whether it is dealing with a difficult parent, leading a team of teachers or managing your workload, coaching gives you the skills to positively deal with the range of challenges a teacher faces.

I will discuss the coaching process in more detail. However, the easiest way to understand it is to consider it as an activity that enables you to explore a challenging aspect of your practice in greater detail. An area of practice that you would like to improve. The job of the coach is to question you in such a way that you are enabled to consider potential solutions for yourself; it is not simply about offering advice. Everybody in the thinking school can benefit from coaching – from the NQT in their very first year to the headteacher with 30 years' experience. Andy Murray is one of the best tennis players in the world, but he employs a coach to enable him to be even better. Coaching is about taking someone from where they currently are in their practice and enabling them to improve.

Coaching skills cannot be developed through a one-day course; they have to be continually developed over time. Through ongoing engagement in coaching, teachers develop both an understanding of the model and an awareness of how to use coaching to develop themselves and team members. As a school leader, I am actively aware of the significant positive impact on all staff and children of working at the centre of a team of teachers who are now experienced coaches. I have been involved in an action learning set (a pure form of coaching that avoids any type of mentoring or advice-giving) for over 15 years and it is one of the most valuable professional or personal learning experiences that I have ever been involved in. It has enabled me to evaluate difficult situations I have faced and arrive at informed actions that develop and improve my practice. It has also given me the skills to effectively self-evaluate and problem-solve in my practice.

Coaching is fundamental to the culture of learning in the school. Were I to discuss the general principles for coaching, I would highlight: its impact on professional learning; its value to staff self-assessment and reflection; its influence on the building of relational trust; its positive impact on our communication with children and parents; and its value in developing the emotional climate across the school. It enables each teacher to understand exactly where they are in their learning, where they need to get to and how best to get there. (Indeed, that is the etymology of the word 'coach' in this sense – a tutor who transports (as in a coach and horses) a student to greater understanding.)

As a headteacher, I can acknowledge that schools are operating in an environment of continual change and need to continually improve. In recent years, the expected standards for children at each Key Stage in primary schools have been raised considerably. In order to respond to these changes, the thinking school requires teachers that are not fixed in their thinking and are equally open to continual individual and collective improvement. For us to achieve well, we need to build increased personal learning capacity in both adults and children. Coaching is at the centre of learning for teachers, helping them to understand their current effectiveness in their roles. Through a trusting partnership with a skilled coach, they are able to focus on their personal learning and arrive at individually contextualised solutions. If all teachers are engaging in coaching, the collective capacity for learning and growth across the school is maximised.

As you become more experienced as a coach, you are stronger in both assessing and developing others and assessing and developing yourself. Coaching is fundamental to what I have described in the thinking school as 'quality change'. Going right back to my conversation with Professor Black all those years ago, quality change can be seen as the antithesis to making knee-jerk reactions. It's when we take the time to deeply reflect upon practice and find solutions to improve children's learning and outcomes. Quality change through coaching is underpinned by teachers having the mindset that we are continually growing and reflecting on our own learning and our impact upon the children each and every day. Coaching enables us to focus on learning rather than teaching.

Through coaching, we are helping our teachers to learn about themselves and their practice. Developing skills of coaching can only enhance our effectiveness as learning-focused leaders.

When to mentor and when to coach

How do we find the balance between mentoring and coaching? The easiest way to distinguish between mentoring and coaching is to remember that mentoring includes the giving of advice. In coaching, we simply question. Within the thinking school, leaders are allocated time for coaching sessions. However, there is no reason why these sessions cannot contain a combination of mentoring and coaching. Coaching also does not have to be restricted to specific sessions that are allocated to it. Once a person has developed good coaching skills, they will be expected to use these skills where appropriate in their professional interactions with colleagues. This can include informal conversations in the corridor.

I see the teachers developing mentoring skills quite naturally in their professional practice; when they encounter colleagues with potential problems, they automatically look to find solutions for them. This is because we see ourselves as part of a caring profession, and we want to help our colleagues. It's also because we don't have the time in our busy working lives for deeper learning-focused conversations. But although we may have solved a problem in the short term, we may not have supported our colleague's enhanced professional learning and understanding. Through coaching questions, we would encourage deeper consideration of the problem. Finding their own solutions will support their learning and build their capacity to self-assess and problem-solve in the future.

Most interactions between colleagues involve a combination of coaching and mentoring, and it is important to distinguish between the two. I regard mentoring as including guidance and advice and associate it with professionals new to their role, such as NQTs or new subject leaders. Coaching relationships do not preclude opportunities to give direct advice. However, it is important to develop pure coaching skills and these are definitely not about giving advice. When developing staff as coaches, I make the distinction between offering advice and asking questions – when in doubt, ask a question! My favourite coaching question is, 'What would you like to see happen?' It is the skill of a coach to listen actively and ask the most thought-provoking question at the right time to challenge the coachee and to empower them to develop their understanding.

It is important that all the staff team are equally committed to the coaching process. It can be a difficult experience and a new way of working. Particularly challenging for both parties is moving away from giving and receiving advice, to asking and receiving questions. School leaders in the thinking school have to be careful to communicate explicitly why you are committed to coaching and its value. You have to commit to its development over time. All of our staff team, including support staff and the office team, took part in a professional learning programme of 30-minute sessions each week for a term. During this time, they developed a theoretical understanding of coaching and were given opportunities to observe and participate in coaching sessions, both as coach and as coachee.

Coaching is the first professional learning activity we engage our NQTs in. We view it as the vehicle to collectively transport the school from where we are now to where we want to be. At an individual level, coaching is about empowering teachers to have the skills to grow for themselves. In hierarchical systems in schools, teachers are often disempowered by constantly being told what to do, and monitored to check they are doing it. They become dependent on affirmation from above; whereas in the thinking school, teachers are supported to question and learn for themselves.

In implementing coaching across the school, we used the GROW model to guide our practice. It was introduced by Whitmore (2009) and colleagues in the 1980s and we found it a relatively straightforward framework to enable the staff team to develop their understanding of the coaching process. As time has gone by and our teachers have developed their expertise as coaches, they have become more flexible in the way they use the model. The GROW model comprises the four key steps in the coaching model:

- **Goals – the coachee's awareness of their aspirations.** The goal stage enables the coachee to consider the area of their learning that they wish to discuss and what their aims are. An example question might be: 'What would you like to be different when you leave this conversation?'

- **Reality – their current situation in relation to those aspirations.** The reality stage is about establishing the level of the coachee's understanding. It is also the stage at which the coach can ask any questions for clarification, such as, 'What is working well right now?'

- **Options – the choices and possibilities available to them.** The options stage is all about inviting the coachee to identify the range of potential options for what they could do. A question might be: 'What possibilities for action can you see?'

- **Will – the actions they commit to undertake to move towards those goals.** The will stage is about identifying the actions the coachee will commit to taking. Having developed their understanding of the current situation, and the choices they have, they commit to key actions. The coach might ask at this stage, 'On a scale of 1–10, how committed and motivated are you to doing it?' The first stage of the next coaching session will be to ask the coachee about how close they are to completing these actions and the outcomes.

Our staff have become more creative and reflective through coaching. If they have a problem, I believe they are less likely to go to colleagues and leaders to have a moan; more likely to come with potential solutions. Through coaching, teachers are empowered to improve constantly; and we want them to empower children in the school in the same way. Coaching makes staff feel valued and listened to. The coaching model includes appreciative enquiry, whereby teachers recognise their strengths and what they do well. They can then think clearly about their current situation as a starting point for improvement.

For many staff at our school, coaching has transformed their practice. There are countless examples to illustrate this and I'm aware that for many of my colleagues, coaching is the most-valued professional learning activity they engage in. One teaching assistant discussed how she altered her mindset when managing a difficult conversation with a parent. She explained how she would previously have reacted negatively to a parent criticising a teacher. On this occasion, following on from what she had learned through coaching, she gave the parent the opportunity to say everything they had to say and just listened. (In coaching, our staff are trained to reflect back to someone exactly what they have said using the same words – so repeating verbatim rather than interpreting. By doing this, we demonstrate that we are actively listening. We also enable the person to hear what they have said in their own words – an experience that doesn't happen very often for most people.) Rather than provoking the parent or worsening the situation, this tactic caused the parent to feel valued and listened to, and her demeanour changed – she was shocked when hearing back the things she said and became more conciliatory. During a PLM, the teaching assistant presented this scenario back to the wider staff team as an example of coaching that had enabled her to deal with a challenging situation in a more positive way than her previous experiences.

In another example, a leader used a coaching conversation to prepare a team leader for having a difficult conversation with a colleague. Coaching is about empowering colleagues to find solutions to challenging situations they are facing. They are far more likely to commit to a solution that they have arrived at for themselves.

A consistent approach is needed to develop a positive culture for coaching in the thinking school. Coaching conversations have to be both authentic and regular, and participants have to believe in them. Their purpose is to build on existing strengths, and develop positive individual dispositions to learning, so that teachers are committed to continual quality change, enhancing the emotional climate in the school.

Summary

This chapter discussed key factors that can affect teacher learning in schools and the need to give teachers the time during the school day and the opportunities to engage in professional learning activities. When designing learning activities that are motivating and engaging for teachers, certain factors are key. Collaborative learning effectively engages teachers and positively affects the learning environment in schools.

Collaboration was extended to consider modelling and sharing practice by all teachers. To develop confident, reflective, learning-focused leaders, we need to constantly model these learning behaviours and skills. We thus improve teaching and children's learning. Coaching, too, is a pillar of the development of individual dispositions to learning and the expansive learning environment in the school. Through coaching, learning-focused leaders become solution-focused and the collective staff team continually critically evaluate practice on a journey of improvement.

Relevant reading

Ball, S. J. (2012) 'The making of a neoliberal academic', *Research in Secondary Education* 2 (1) pp. 29–31.

Leithwood, K., Day, C., Sammons, P., Harris, A. and Hopkins, D. (2006) *Seven strong claims about successful school leadership*. Nottingham: National College for School Leadership.

Whitmore, J. (2009) *Coaching for performance: growing human potential and purpose: the principles and practice of coaching and leadership*. London: Quercus.

Reflective questions

1. How would you describe the culture for teacher professional learning at your school?

2. What opportunities do teachers at your school have to engage in collaborative professional learning?

3. What factors affect teacher engagement in professional learning in your school?

4. Are teachers able to choose the topics for their own professional learning?

5. How many opportunities do you think teachers have to engage in modelling and sharing of practice?

6. To what extent is coaching practised at your school? Is it something that you would like to develop? How do you feel your staff would respond to it?

Chapter 6

Conclusions

I wrote this book because I wanted to share the findings of my research and experience in creating and developing the 'thinking school'. What I believe is unique about the thinking school is its ability to evaluate and reflect upon current practice, trying out changes to inform future practice. The collective knowledge and understanding of teaching and learning is used to continually improve practice. The activities in the dynamic learning community are interdependent and, applied together, they will have a powerful effect on teacher learning and pupil learning. Apply these activities in a culture of high trust and high challenge and members of staff will value their own learning, their children's learning and their colleagues' learning.

There is sufficient evidence to indicate that we need to think anew about what models for teacher learning are effective. If national policy in the UK is to facilitate greater opportunities for teacher engagement in research and professional learning, schools need leaders who can provide expansive opportunities for teacher learning. We must reconceptualise the role of the teacher, and place professional learning at the centre. Likewise the role of school leaders must have leadership of teacher learning at the centre. By developing learning-focused leaders at my current school, we create future headteachers who will lead their own thinking schools.

Whole-school teacher learning will enable teachers to participate in collaborative, contextualised professional learning activities. I believe that this will lead to a more motivating and engaging professional learning experience and enhanced self-efficacy and confidence amongst teachers. It is so important to the future success of our profession that teachers have positive early experiences in their careers. They should feel that they are in a profession where their learning is valued and where they are able to continue to grow and develop.

The concept of professional learning communities within and between schools warrants explicit promotion at a national level and needs to be valued through the inspection framework. Essentially, schools and school leaders should be held accountable for the learning outcomes of not only children but teachers too. The key findings discussed in this book have been replicated in two recent wide-scale studies of the teaching profession. The Coe et al. study on what makes great teaching (2014) highlighted the significance of sustained professional learning opportunities over time, the value of supportive professional learning environments, and the extent to which these learning opportunities were influenced by school leaders:

> 'Teachers working in schools with more supportive professional [learning] environments continued to improve significantly after three years … Sustained professional learning is most likely to result when … an environment of professional learning and support is promoted by the school's leadership.' (p. 5)

An international study by Schleicher in 2015 on the teaching profession describes how teacher learning approaches have remained the same despite constant changes to conceptions of pupil learning and the skills required for students to contribute effectively to society. Schleicher argues that three key ingredients are required to create a responsive 21-century school:

1. Teachers who are confident in their ability to teach

2. Willingness to innovate

3. Strong school leaders who establish the conditions in their school that enables the former two ingredients to flourish (p. 9)

Schleicher makes the importance of leadership and collaborative learning clear. Both his study and that of Coe and colleagues highlight the value of collaborative learning activities such as peer learning and team-teaching. We know that this is not characteristic of the professional learning opportunities most teachers in primary schools in England now experience. Ball (2013) rightly argues that education in the UK requires a new kind of informed teacher who is committed to collaborative learning. Establishing the dynamic learning community in schools places teacher learning at the centre of the thinking school, where it can transform children's learning and outcomes. I believe it will promote the wellbeing of teachers and enable the accelerated development of informed, confident and innovative practitioners. They will be led by learning-focused leaders and develop the skills of learning-focused leaders themselves.

As evidenced in this book, I have developed an understanding of the factors that I believe can enable schools to provide the best possible learning experiences for teachers. This understanding is important to me because I wish to enable children to have the best possible learning environments and experiences. This is a personal aspiration for me in that I want all children to see themselves as learners and to believe that they can be successful and make a positive difference to our world. I want every child to have an excellent educational experience and to be taught by the types of reflective, informed and humble teachers that I currently have the privilege to be working with. We have to believe that education can enable us to move to a better world, and we have to ensure that our profession is more highly valued.

In my introduction, I discussed that most teachers join the profession because they want to make a positive difference to children's lives. It is up to school leaders to take ultimate responsibility to design a learning climate that enables teachers to do this. Crucially, it is about enabling your team of staff to concentrate their energies to be the best that they can be. I am sure that I will continue to learn over the coming years and adapt, develop and improve the activities of the dynamic learning community at the heart of the thinking school. I will also consider how we can move from a thinking school to a thinking schools system.

Relevant reading

Ball, S. J. (2013) *Education, justice and democracy: the struggle over ignorance and opportunity.* London: Centre for Labour and Social Studies.

Coe, R., Aloisi, C., Higgins, S. and Major, L. E. (2014) *What makes great teaching? Review of the underpinning research.* London: The Sutton Trust.

Schleicher, A. (2015) *Schools for 21-century learners: strong leaders, confident teachers, innovative approaches.* Paris: OECD Publishing.

Reflective questions

1. How do you think other teachers in your school would respond if they read this book?

2. What are your plans for developing teacher learning at your school in the next six months?

3. Where would you like your school to be in five years' time? Where would you like to be? What are your personal aspirations in your role?

4. To what extent could the development of a thinking school enable you to meet the future challenges facing your school?

References

Alexander, R. J. (2017) *Towards dialogic teaching: rethinking classroom talk*. 5th edn. York: Dialogos.

Ball, S. J. (2012) 'The making of a neoliberal academic', *Research in Secondary Education* 2 (1) pp. 29–31.

Ball, S. J. (2013) *Education, justice and democracy: the struggle over ignorance and opportunity*. London: Centre for Labour and Social Studies.

Billett, S. (2006) 'Constituting the workplace curriculum', *Journal of Curriculum Studies* 38 (1) pp. 31–48.

Black, P. and Wiliam, D. (1998) *Inside the black box: raising standards through classroom assessment*. London: GL Assessment.

Coe, R., Aloisi, C., Higgins, S. and Major, L. E. (2014) *What makes great teaching? Review of the underpinning research*. London: The Sutton Trust.

Cordingley, P., Higgins, S., Greany, T., Buckler, N., Coles-Jordan, D., Crisp, B., Saunders, L. and Coe, R. (2015) *Developing great teaching: lessons from the international reviews into effective professional development*. London: Teacher Development Trust.

Elliot, J. (2007) 'Assessing the quality of action research', *Research Papers in Education* 22 (2) pp. 229–246.

Eraut, M. (2004) 'Informal learning in the workplace', *Studies in Continuing Education* 26 (2) pp. 247–273.

Eurydice (2015) *The teaching profession in Europe: practices, perceptions, and policies*. Luxembourg: Publications Office of the European Union.

Evans, K., Hodkinson, P., Rainbird, H and Unwin, L. (2006) *Improving workplace learning*. Abingdon: Routledge.

Fuller, A. and Unwin, L. (2004) 'Expansive learning environments: integrating personal and organizational development' in Rainbird, H., Fuller, A. and Munro, A. (eds) *Workplaces learning in context*. London: Routledge, pp. 126–144.

Fuller, A., Hodkinson, H., Hodkinson, P. and Unwin, L. (2005) 'Learning as peripheral participation in communities of practice: a reassessment of key concepts in workplace learning', *British Educational Research Journal* 31 (1) pp. 49–68.

Fuller, A. and Unwin, L. (2006) 'Expansive and restrictive learning environments' in Evans, L., Hodkinson, P., Rainbird, H. and Unwin, L. (eds) *Improving workplace learning*. London: Routledge, pp. 27–48.

General Teaching Council for England (2007) *Making CPD better: bringing together research about CPB*. London: GTCE.

Hoban, G. F. (2002) *Teacher learning for educational change*. Buckingham: Open University Press.

Hodkinson, P. and Hodkinson, H. (2004) 'The significance of individuals' dispositions in workplace learning: a case study of two teachers', *Journal of Education and Work* 17 (2) pp. 167–182.

Hodkinson, H. and Hodkinson, P. (2005) 'Improving schoolteachers' workplace learning', *Research Papers in Education* 20 (2) pp. 109–131.

Kraft, M. A. and Papay, J. P. (2014) 'Do supportive professional environments promote teacher development? Explaining heterogeneity in returns to teaching experience', *Educational Evaluation and Policy Analysis* 36 (4) pp. 476–500.

Lave, J. and Wenger, E. (1991) *Situated learning*. Cambridge: Cambridge University Press.

Leithwood, K., Day, C., Sammons, P., Harris, A. and Hopkins, D. (2006) *Seven strong claims about successful school leadership*. Nottingham: National College for School Leadership.

McNiff, J. and Whitehead, J. (2005) *Action research for teachers: a practical guide*. London: David Fulton.

Nonaka, I. and Takeuchi, H. (1995) *The knowledge-creating company: how Japanese companies create the dynamics of innovation*. New York, NY: Oxford University Press.

Robinson, V. (2011) *Student-centered leadership*. San Francisco, CA: Jossey-Bass.

Schleicher, A. (2015) *Schools for 21-century learners: strong leaders, confident teachers, innovative approaches*. Paris: OECD Publishing.

Stenhouse, L. (1975) *An introduction to curriculum research and development*. London: Heinemann.

UCET (2011) *UCET annual report 2011: educating the UK's educators*. London: UCEL Institute of Education.

Wenger, E. (2008) *Communities of practice: a brief introduction*. Available at: www.goo.gl/SAUovq (Accessed 28th November 2018)

Whitmore, J. (2009) *Coaching for performance: growing human potential and purpose: the principles and practice of coaching and leadership*. London: Quercus.